EX
RI
CHRISTIA
TESTAME

The Exploration Series published by Paternoster Press and Open Book

1998 Interpreting God's Plan: Biblical Theology and the Pastor
R.J. Gibson (Gen. Ed.)

EXPLORATIONS 12
RIPE FOR HARVEST: CHRISTIAN MISSION IN THE NEW TESTAMENT AND IN OUR WORLD

General Editor
R. J. Gibson

paternoster press

OPENBOOK
PUBLISHERS

Printed by arrangement with Openbook Publishers,
205 Halifax Street, Adelaide, South Australia 5000
openbook@peg.apc.org

First published in 2000 by Paternoster Press

06 05 04 03 02 01 00 7 6 5 4 3 2 1

Paternoster Press is an imprint of Paternoster Publishing,
P.O. Box 300, Carlisle, Cumbria, CA3 0QS, UK
www.paternoster-publishing.com

British Library Cataloguing in Publication Data
A catalogue record for this book is available from the British Library
ISBN 0-85364-980-4

Cover Design by Mainstream, Lancaster, UK
Typeset by WestKey Ltd, Falmouth, Cornwall, UK
Printed in Great Britain by
Omnia Books Ltd, Glasgow

Contents

Contents

Preface

Evangelical Christians are prominent in the modern missionary movement. Our zeal and efforts have not always been accompanied by sufficient theological reflection. We do not make the contribution to missiology that the strength of our commitment suggests that we should. The faculty of Moore College hopes that the chapters in this book will engage important issues in a biblical way and so strengthen the cause of the Lord Jesus Christ. We hope that they will be a useful resource for those who are engaged in mission. To this end we have addressed such matters as the responsibility of all Christians for mission, pluralism and the gospel, the theological foundations of church growth, and the role of the Spirit. In particular we welcome the important contribution of Michael Raiter, who used the opportunity to give his inaugural address as the Head of the Department of Mission at Moore College. In doing so he laid the foundation for what we as a College mean by mission, and how we intend to urge forward the great work that the Lord has given us to do.

The appointment of Michael Raiter was the culmination of almost a decade of prayer and planning. The College is committed to the view that mission ought to be high on the Christian agenda. Many of our graduates are serving in cross-cultural situations and the normal expectation of current students is that they will be involved in the front line of evangelistic mission, wherever they are placed. We had long recognised that mission deserved a far higher profile in the formal life of the College, and that the way to accomplish this was to have a department dedicated to the subject and to find a worthy person to be its representative. Funding was made available through the generosity of an individual, and the Department commenced its full time work in 1997.

The papers in this volume were presented at the 1997 School of Theology as a way of inaugurating the new work. We are very much aware that the whole field of missions is marked both by theological controversy and by theological weakness. On the one hand, there are issues to do with the very significance of mission itself, the meaning of the gospel for the contemporary world and the question of the obligation of Christians to preach an exclusive message in a pluralist environment. On the other hand, there are theories of how mission should be practised which seem to owe more to secular than to theological thought. If we are to be involved in mission in a way that is obedient to the Lord, brings honour to his name and blessing to his people, we must study the Scriptures and give deep thought to the issues that confront us.

Peter F. Jensen
Principal
Moore College
September, 1998

Abbreviations

EMQ	*Evangelical Missions Quarterly*
ANCL	*The Ante-Nicene Christian Library*
ET	*English Translation*
IBMR	*International Bulletin of Missionary Research*
IRM	*International Review of Mission*
IVP	Inter-Varsity Press
JSNT	*Journal for the Study of the New Testament*
JSP	*Journal for the Study of the Pseudepigrapha*
LXX	Septuagint
NABPR	National Association of Baptist Professors of Religion
NICNT	New International Commentary on the New Testament
NIV	New International Version
NRSV	New Revised Standard Version
NT	New Testament
OT	Old Testament
RTR	*Reformed Theological Review*
SCM	Student Christian Movement
SPCK	Society for the Promotion Christian Knowledge
TDNT	*Theological Dictionary of the New Testament*
WCC	World Council of Churches

1

Following Jesus and Fishing for People: Evangelistic Mission in the Third Millennium

Peter Bolt

Synopsis

Responding to the call to place evangelistic mission on firmer biblical theological foundations, this article begins with the premise that the Gospels (and Acts) arose from the work of mission in order to support the work of mission. As such, these narratives ought to play a key role in the foundations for evangelistic mission.

The Gospels speak of historical events associated with Jesus which are of immense theological significance for the world. Given that many have been sceptical about the historicity of much of the Gospels' material, it is observed that they are written with a real-world flavour. Even the most sceptical agree that Jesus restricted his own mission to Israel and yet called twelve disciples who then formed the spearhead of the new Christian movement which exercised an aggressive missionary campaign to the Gentile world. This movement was motivated by a theological understanding of who Jesus was and what he had done. By narrating the story of Jesus in a way that demonstrates his theological significance, the Gospels motivate their readers towards evangelistic mission.

An examination of the Gospels shows that their readers are joined to the mission of Jesus by way of the mission of the apostles, whose word is now enshrined in the NT. Since the resurrection, Jesus' mission continues through the proclamation of the apostolic word which centres upon the forgiveness of sins. The hearers of that word are not only objects of his mission, as part of the harvest field, but also instruments of his mission, as they believe the apostolic word and proclaim it further.

Evangelistic mission in the third millennium

The malaise of a missionary movement?

From the very beginning the Christian movement was recognised as a missionary movement which 'turned the world upside down' (Acts 17:6) with its evangelistic message.[1] But as we face the third millennium, perhaps we can be forgiven for asking whether the enemies of the Christian churches still feel threatened by the preaching of the gospel turning the world upside down. The aggressive missionary movement, which took the first-century world by storm, appears to be suffering something of a malaise.

Others are no doubt glad that the early fervour has disappeared. Should we speak of mission at all, given the overtones of cultural imperialism? Should we speak of dialogue, not proclamation? Should we be engaged in the alleviation of social problems instead of, or as well as, or alongside, the work of evangelistic mission? Come to think of it, is *evangelistic* mission appropriate at all in our pluralistic world? Is it appropriate for *all* Christian people? Shouldn't it be seen as one vocation amongst many, and shouldn't the church encourage all Christians to pursue their own particular vocation for the good of society, leaving the work of evangelism to those who have that calling?[2]

---

[1] For modern scholars who concur with the ancient testimony see, for example, those cited in D. J. Bosch, 'Reflections on Biblical Models of Mission', in J. M. Phillips and R. T. Coote, eds, *Towards the Twentyfirst Century in Christian Mission. Essays in Honor of Gerald H. Anderson* (Grand Rapids: Eerdmans, 1993) 177.

[2] Cf. the broad Anglican viewpoint in which the 'Anglican impulse' is 'bearing witness to that Christian faith and the presence of God in the world'; 'The central focus, direction and goal of Christian discipleship, is our civic vocation among

However, in the face of the malaise of this once-great missionary movement, some voices are calling for greater efforts in evangelistic mission in all quarters and from all quarters:

> Even in Australia, the need of the hour is the missionary; indeed each person in pastoral ministry needs to be a missionary.[3]

This particular voice has even led to the establishment of a department of mission here at Moore, which must be a bold statement that it will continue to be relevant to have such a department in the new millennium. How can this be justified?

Motivating evangelistic mission

Mission may imply different things to different people. In some quarters a mission is where the homeless receive a bowl of soup. For most, it implies an extended term of service in a land not your own,[4] whether that service consists of acting in the capacity of evangelist or Bible teacher, or 'secular' professional. For some time, there have also been those calling upon Christians to view every land as a mission-field, and themselves as missionaries wherever they may be—overseas trips or not![5]

---

[2] (*continued*) our fellow citizens. It is this concentration on social vocation, which gives significance to what is done in Church. Church activity is not an end in itself, but rather a means to the worshipping of God through the fulfilment of our Christian vocation in the society and in the world in which God has placed us', B. N. Kaye, 'Theology for Life in a Plural Society', *Lucas* 19 and 20 (1995–96) 204.

[3] P. F. Jensen, 'Maturing the Mind: Intellectual Attainment and Theological Education', *RTR* 55/3 (1996) 118.

[4] Bosch, 'Reflections', 176. I have added the professional's service. Bosch's focus is on 'winning converts and planting churches'. He dates this view of mission to the Jesuits of the 16th century, and shows how easily such a view came to be entangled with colonialisation.

[5] L. Newbigin issued such a call in 1956. He claimed that the church's mission is none other than that of Christ himself and the apostles, which meant that mission consisted not so much in the crossing of geographical frontiers as in *crossing the frontier between faith in Christ as Lord and unbelief*. A missionary is therefore anyone who is sent to make Christ known among those who do not know him, whether the journey is short or long.

I am reliant upon the summary of his position paper to the International Missionary Council in J. A. Scherer, 'Mission Theology', in Phillips and Coote,

Given the malaise of our missionary movement, and the differing responses to that malaise, how do we motivate people towards mission—especially evangelistic mission? In the past, this has been done through appeal to certain 'missionary texts' gleaned from the pages of the Bible, most frequently from the pages of the NT[6]—it was thought that the OT's 'particularism' negated its relevance for the work of mission. It is probably fair to say that, since the time of William Carey,[7] the edifice of Christian missions has rested largely on the cornerstone provided by one solitary text, namely, Matthew's 'Great Commission' (Matt 28:18–20).[8] An appeal to this text—and often with little regard for its context as the final scene of Matthew's Gospel[9]—has been considered sufficient to establish the work of mission.[10]

Such an approach can actually be counter-productive for those seeking to motivate people towards mission. Unfortunately in the number-crunching climate of the modern world, exegesis is done by democracy as well. With our tally boards at the ready, it can be asked whether evangelistic mission is such a big deal, if the NT must be squeezed so hard to produce such a small yield of verses in its favour. It could be noted that the NT only infrequently commands all Christian people to

---

[5] (*continued*) 197. A careful exegesis of Matt 28:18–20 enables P. T. O'Brien, 'The Great Commission of Matthew 28:18–20. A Missionary Mandate or Not?', *RTR* 35 (1976) 73, 78, to make the same point.

[6] Bosch, 'Reflections', 175–176.

[7] Noted by Bosch, 'Reflections', 176, and M. Arias and A. Johnson, *The Great Commission: Biblical Models for Evangelism* (Nashville: Abingdon, 1992), 16, who draw upon L. Newbigin, *Mission in Christ's Way: Bible Studies* (Geneva: WCC, 1987), 32. In 1792 Carey published *An Enquiry into the Obligations of Christians to use Means for the Conversion of the Heathen* in which he argued that Matthew's final command was binding upon all. For a brief look at the history of the 'Great Commission', see O'Brien, 'Great Commission', 66–67.

[8] Cf Mark 16:15,16 which may be another version of the Great Commission.

[9] Arias and Johnson, *Biblical Models*, 11, complain that: 'usually the "Great Commission" is quoted and interpreted out of context, most of the time unrelated to the full content of the [G]ospels of which the commission is the climax. It is amazing how little exegesis goes on in the usual articles and messages on the subject.'

[10] Arias and Johnson, *Biblical Models*, 15–16, suggest that this latter assumption was firmly set in place by the Edinburgh conference in 1910.

evangelise.[11] It could even be claimed that such commands were solely meant for a select group,[12] such as the apostles,[13] or Jewish Christians, or some other first-century group, not for Christians of later generations, certainly not those at the end of the twentieth century. Under such an exegetical method, the more the motivation for mission rests upon the Great Commission, the shakier the whole edifice becomes.

The search for the movement's foundations

In view of the various discussions and debates about mission, and the evident problems with some of the methods used for motivation, there have been many calls for mission to be set upon better foundations. This search for better foundations has been going on for some time, and no doubt 'will be as important in the twenty-first century as it has been in the past'— if not more so.[14]

However, as we face the third millennium with all the challenges that it may bring to life in general and the Christian life in particular, if Christian people are to be motivated towards the work of mission at all, then this motivation will

---

[11] This problem was raised, for example, in K. A. Mascord, 'Equipping the Local Church for Mission', in *Explorations 7, Exploring The Missionary Church,* ed. B. G. Webb, (Homebush West, NSW: ANZEA, 1993) 125–150. This argument has also surfaced in the recent debate amongst Sydney Anglicans over whether all Christians should evangelise. See further the letters and articles in *Southern Cross* from Oct 97 onwards by K. Mason, D. Mansfield, J. Dickson and R. Blight. In 1997 James D. Bates also circulated a general letter amongst Sydney Anglican Clergy which invoked the same argument.

[12] O'Brien, 'Great Commission', 66, addresses this problem in regard to Matt 28:18–20.

[13] This was the Reformers' and the majority of 17th century theologians' view of Matt 28:18–20; see O'Brien, 'Great Commission', 66–67.

[14] Bosch, 'Reflections', 175. A. J. Bailyes, 'Evangelical and Ecumenical Understandings of Mission', *IRM* 85/339 (Oct 1996), 485–503, has argued that from the 1980s to the 1991 Canberra convention, the divide between evangelism and social concern, reflected in evangelical and ecumenical debates of the late 60's/early 70's, began to narrow. The 'evangelical stresses the need for social concern still in the overarching logical priority of evangelism and the ecumenical strongly affirming the need for proclamation of the gospel with a call to conversion for salvation'. Yet, despite identifying a convergence, he identifies the need for a better theological underpinning (p 497).

need to be profound. Many have been calling for such firm foundations to be laid, not simply by sinking a couple of piers into the mud by way of isolated proof-texts, but by uncovering the solid bedrock of the whole thrust of Scripture.[15] Bosch puts the case starkly:

> Our point of departure should not be the contemporary enterprise we seek to justify, but the biblical sense of what being sent into the world signifies. It also means that, however important single biblical texts may (seem to) be, the validity of mission should not be deduced from isolated sayings but from the thrust of the central message of Scripture. In other words, either mission—properly understood—lies at the heart of the biblical message or it is so peripheral to that message that we need not be overly concerned with it.[16]

Bosch is correct to put the alternatives so strongly. If evangelistic mission is addressed merely by one or two verses on the periphery of the Scriptures, then it would be right to give those verses the small amount of interest that good balance allows. This would then properly relegate the whole task of evangelistic mission to those who are particularly gifted or concerned for it, or, if it does concern us all to some extent, to make sure that it does not get out of balance with the other myriad concerns of life. But if mission lies at the heart of the biblical message, then the apparently small number of verses which explicitly command evangelistic endeavours become immensely important as the tip of an iceberg moving along under the biblical theological impetus of the entire plan of God throughout the ages.[17] In this

---

[15] Attempts at a recovery of a biblical theology of mission are documented by Bosch, 'Reflections', 177–180; Scherer, 'Mission Theology'; J. B. Green, ' "Proclaiming Repentance and Forgiveness of Sins to All Nations": A Biblical Perspective on the Church's Mission', in A. G. Padgett, ed., *The Mission of the Church in Methodist Perspective. The World is My Parish* (Lewiston: Edwin Mellen, 1992), 13–23. Peter O'Brien and Andreas Köstenberger are currently writing a biblical theology of mission.

[16] Bosch, 'Reflections', 177.

[17] Cf. the discussion in E. Schweizer, 'The Significance of Eschatology in the Teaching of Jesus', in W. H. Gloer, ed., *Eschatology and the New Testament. Essays*

case, evangelistic mission ought to be not only the foundation for the Christian movement, but also the overarching framework within which all else in life gets its bearings. Mission could then properly be regarded as the super-ordinate goal which provides the rationale and the direction for everything that properly occupies Christian people, groups and churches. Being 'close to the heartbeat of the biblical tradition',[18] mission would become crucial for understanding Christian discipleship.

Discovery of the foundations will also provide the answers to the many questions being asked about mission, such as: whether it is still appropriate; what is its nature?; who ought to be involved in it?; and so on. In addition, because this world belongs to God, an understanding of mission which rests upon God's plans through the ages also provides a bridge to our world.

> This great work will only be accomplished by those who are prepared to understand their own message at depth, and understand their own society at similar depth. Those who understand the Bible well will possess an enormously important key to the understanding of the world.[19]

It is the contention of this paper, that the four Gospels (and Acts) go a long way towards providing proper biblical theological foundations for mission as it was in the first century and as it ought to be in the twenty-first century.

---

[17] *(continued) in Honor of George Raymond Beasley-Murray* (Peabody: Hendrickson, 1988), in which Schweizer argues that even where there is a lack of an explicit theology (in his essay, eschatology) this may be because it is present at the level of 'unquestionable presuppositions'. 'This shows how fatal it would be to interpret the lack of explicit statements about indubitable presuppositions as a sign of their relative insignificance in which they are understood as an elective rather than the compulsory element of belief' (p. 8); 'it is clear that there are very often assumptions that are not articulated and yet are very central to the original author' (p. 10); 'In some way, faith is . . . much more dependent on underground convictions that impose themselves upon the believer as a self-evident truth than on ideas that can be manipulated by others, strung together in a logical order and buttressed by arguments. This means that we should take all the underlying "taken-for-granteds" even more seriously than the articulated dogmas' (pp. 10–11).

[18] Green, 'Proclaiming', 15.

[19] Jensen, 'Maturing', 118.

The Gospels and mission

Gospels as 'missionary tracts'

Although it has not been usual to do so, it can be argued that each of the Gospels arose from the setting of mission,[20] in order to support the work of mission. The gospel was written down, not in order to correct some problem or other—as if the Gospels were written out of the same kind of motivation as, say, the Epistle to the Galatians or Colossians—but because the events of which they speak were worth the telling.[21] By presenting the stories of Jesus, they would have functioned as evangelistic documents for those who did not yet believe and, for those who believed already, as motivators towards the work of evangelism. As 'missionary tracts', in this sense, the Gospels ought to have a foundational role in discussions of mission.

The Gospels and Jesus

Although it may sound obvious, it must be said that the Gospels are about Jesus. They are not books about the church, or books about ourselves, but they are about Jesus. Although the content of the Gospels will have massive implication for churches and for individuals, the Gospels should be read in the first place to get in touch with what they say about Jesus. Since Jesus is the founder of the Christian missionary movement, an examination of his mission as portrayed by the Gospels ought to have a foundational role in discussions of mission.

Narratives of theologically significant events

The Gospels support the work of mission. They persuade not by the statement of a creed, or a confession; nor by isolated

---

[20] Arias, in Arias and Johnson, *Biblical Models*, 13, endorses the point, noting that the Gospels arose from 'the real context of the churches and their mission'; and that (on Matthew), this 'Gospel was written out of mission, for mission' (p. 17).

[21] See R. Bauckham, 'For Whom Were the Gospels Written?', in R. Bauckham, ed., *The Gospels for All Christians: Rethinking the Gospel Audiences* (Grand Rapids: Eerdmans, 1998) 9–48. P. Oxy 1381 provides an apt analogy, in which a man writes the story of the God Asklepios as an act of thanks for his own salvation, so that he might commend the God and his salvation to others. See D. R. Cartlidge and D. L. Dungan, eds, *Documents for the Study of the Gospels* (Minneapolis: Fortress, ^{2}1994) 121–124.

theological statements; nor by collecting together a bunch of wise and/or dominical sayings, but by means of a narrative. They are narratives of theologically significant events. In other words, they persuade through the presentation of complex portraits of Jesus (narrative), who is always related in some way to the world (events), and to the movement explaining him to the world (theological significance).

The events and the mission

The Christian mission is grounded in events of the real world. However, as is well known, this claim to historicity has been under sustained attack for a long time. It is therefore worthwhile to make a few comments about how the Christian mission is grounded in real historical events.

Real world flavour

The Gospels depict the events about which they write with a real-world flavour. Each writer in their own way and to varying degrees, depicts the story of Jesus as occurring within the normal political, geographical, and social conditions of the times. For sure, the miraculous events are unusual, although they are not without analogy within Israel's history or the ancient world, and they are probably more problematic for the post-enlightenment modern world (and perhaps not so problematic for the post-modern world?).

It must also be said that there is nothing unusual about the people who are assisted by Jesus in the miracle stories. This group of people with all their illnesses and afflictions are just as much a sample of life in the ancient world as those found in the case-studies of the great doctor Hippocrates. As such, these individual units which contribute so much to the Gospels, provide a genuine slice-of-life from the ancient world. These are not presented as mere characters set within a moralistic framework, as people to whom the Gospel readers ought to aspire, but as real people, with names, addresses, and genuine human needs; people like those the early Gospel readers would see everyday, and amongst whom they would count themselves already. They are not ideal characters invented for the story, but are characters within the story who provide a genuine overlap between the story of Jesus and the real world of the readers.[22]

Jesus' death is also set against the political processes of the day, and even his resurrection—for all its manifold claims to the miraculous—is explained by the Gospels with all the marks of a this-worldly realism.

Real world resurrection

The resurrection of Jesus Christ stands at the centre of the Christian mission. Without the resurrection, there would be no mission. As we shall see below, the resurrection of Jesus is of great theological importance, but at this point we need to note that the NT also regards the resurrection as an event which occurred in the real world: a real man from Nazareth, at a certain place, and at a certain time, came back to life again, leaving an empty tomb and showing himself to a select group of people. The reason the apostles entrusted with the role of bearing witness to his resurrection had to be those who were with Jesus from the beginning (Luke 24:36–43, 48–49; Acts 1:3, 21–22; 10:41–43; John 15:27) is presumably so they could testify to the fact that the risen Jesus was the Jesus of Nazareth they had known over many years. They could verify the resurrection was a real event in the real world.[23]

It is completely understandable that many find the resurrection hard to believe, since it runs counter to every shred of evidence in our mortal world and is an event which is unique. But that is the very point. The NT message proclaims that one man, Jesus of Nazareth, rose from the dead, which makes him enormously significant. It was that real event in the real world that gave rise to the mission.

---

[22] I have explored Mark's collection of 'case studies' at length in P. G. Bolt, ' "Do you not care that we are perishing?" Jesus' Defeat of Death and Mark's Early Readers', (Unpublished Ph.D. thesis; King's College, London, 1997).

[23] See further my 'Mission and Witness', in I. H. Marshall and D. G. Peterson, eds, *The Theology of Acts* (Carlisle and Grand Rapids: Paternoster and Eerdmans, 1997) 191–214.

Real world mission

Many are not prepared to take the Gospels at face value as describing what actually happened. It is currently fashionable to propose models for understanding who Jesus 'really' was (as distinct from the portrait painted by the Gospels). It is incumbent upon any proposed model to take into account the generally acknowledged facts and seek to explain them in the best possible way. When it comes to the facts relating to mission, it may be the Gospels themselves provide the best solution.

There are at least three things that even the most sceptical acknowledge as historical fact which relate to the topic of mission.

Jesus and Israel

It is widely agreed that Jesus restricted himself to a ministry within the borders of Israel, although he did have the occasional contact with Gentiles.[24]

In terms of the shape of his ministry to Israel, there are also several items that would be acknowledged as being on firm historical ground. Jesus spoke about the kingdom of God. He gained the reputation for being a wonder-worker, and, although many would dismiss a lot of his miracles out of hand, many are prepared to concede that he was an exorcist and a healer. He ended his time amongst Israel through being crucified at the hands of the Romans.

Jesus and the Twelve

Another historically reliable fact, even to the most sceptical, is that Jesus called twelve disciples.[25] Here the number twelve is

---

[24] M. Davies and E. P. Sanders, *Studying the Synoptic Gospels* (London and Philadelphia: SCM and Trinity Press International, 1989) 305: 'The principal point about the Historical Jesus, which can be proved beyond reasonable doubt, is that he launched his own mission to the people of Israel'; cf p 308. Sanders, *Jesus and Judaism* (London and Philadelphia: SCM and Fortress, 1985) 11, lists as point 4 of those items resting upon the most secure evidence that Jesus restricted his activity to Israel.

[25] Sanders, *Jesus*, 11, lists (point 3) amongst those items resting upon the most secure evidence that Jesus called disciples and spoke of there being twelve; cf 98–100.

important,[26] for it has symbolic significance relating to the twelve tribes of Israel and fits well with Jewish eschatological expectations that the future would see Israel restored and renewed.

How is this fact to be explained? Why did he assemble this team? What was their purpose? What did he have in mind? Just as Jesus restricted his own ministry to Israel, he also initially restricted theirs to Israel as well, but was this a temporary measure? How did he perceive their future role?[27]

Jesus and the Gentile mission

The third thing which is acknowledged as being fundamental historical fact is that Jesus founded a movement which was intensely missionary, practically from its inception.[28] 'The overwhelming impression is that Jesus started a movement which *came to see the Gentile mission as a logical extension of itself.*'[29]

This is all the more remarkable for the fact that the Christian movement was almost certainly the first missionary movement to hit the ancient world. This opinion has been strongly asserted in recent times, in place of an older scholarly assumption which has come under severe attack. For a long time, NT scholarship had assumed that the Christian mission rode on the crest of the wave generated by a previous period of Jewish missionary activity. This assumption gained great scholarly respectability at the turn of the century in Adolf von Harnack's examination of Christian mission in the first three centuries.[30] The assumption was then perpetuated throughout the course of this century under the continued influence of Harnack's book, as well as that

---

[26] Sanders, *Jesus*, 101, talks of the 'historicity of a symbol'; cf 102 for Jesus using it symbolically.

[27] Sanders, *Jesus*, 105–106.

[28] Sanders, *Jesus*, 91, The beginning of Jesus' activity, with John the Baptist, and its outcome in the Gentile mission are most secure; set in the context of Jewish eschatological expectations. See also pp 330–331 for the same framework.

[29] Sanders, *Jesus*, 220, who argues that no Christian group objected to the Gentile mission. For the contrary view, see C. K. Barrett, 'The Gentile Mission as an Eschatological Phenomenon', in Gloer ed., *Eschatology*, 65–67.

[30] A. von Harnack, *The Expansion of Christianity in the First Three Centuries* (tr. J. Moffatt; London: Wiliams & Norgate, 1904).

of other important scholarly works, such as the *TDNT*,[31] and also through influential scholars like Joachim Jeremias. In 1956 Jeremias epitomised this point of view, when he opened his book *Jesus' Promise to the Nations* with these words:

> At the time of Jesus' appearance an unparalleled period of missionary activity was in progress in Israel.[32]

He argued that this Jewish mission had been in existence since at least the Maccabean period, and that it was connected with the rise of the Jewish Diaspora. It was also

> a wholly new phenomenon: Judaism was the first great missionary religion to make its appearance in the Mediterranean world.[33]

He then set the rise of Christianity in the context of this Jewish mission to the nations, claiming that

> this development reached its climax in the lifetime of Jesus and the apostles.[34]

However, a new consensus is emerging that there is no real evidence for such a Jewish mission; apparently it did not exist. For sure, there were some elements of Jewish eschatological expectations which gave a positive place for the Gentiles, but any influx of the Gentiles was expected to occur in the last days and there is no evidence that the Jewish people saw any need to hurry things up at all through an active missionary campaign.[35] When active Jewish mission did emerge in the latter part of the

---

[31] G. Kittel, ed., *Theological Dictionary of the New Testament* (10 Vols.; tr., G. Bromiley; Eerdmans, ET 1964–1976).

[32] J. Jeremias, *Jesus' Promise to the Nations* (London: SCM, ET 1958, 1967, [German: 1956, 1959]) 11.

[33] Jeremias, *Promise*, 11.

[34] Jeremias, *Promise*, 11.

[35] Jeremias, *Promise*, 56; cf Barrett, 'Gentile Mission', 67; Sanders, *Jesus*, 218; T. L. Donaldson, 'Proselytes or "Righteous Gentiles"? The Status of Gentiles in Eschatological Pilgrimage Patterns of Thought', *JSP* 7 (1990) 3–27. A. T. Kraabel, 'Immigrants, Exiles, Expatriates, and Missionaries', in L. Bormann, K. del Tredici, A. Standhartinger, eds, *Religious Propaganda and Missionary Competition in the New Testament World. Essays Honoring Dieter Georgi* (Leiden: Brill, 1994) 71–88.

first century, it appears to have been as a reaction to the aggressive Christian missions amongst the Jewish people and the god-fearers.[36]

If there was no Jewish mission prior to this time, this means that Jesus spawned the world's first aggressively missionary movement. There is no doubt that it was hugely successful, swept like a tidal wave across the ancient world and its effects have been felt across the world even down to the modern day. If Jesus restricted himself to Israel, and yet spawned this great missionary movement, what accounts for its origins? Why were his followers convinced that the events which had occurred surrounding Jesus Christ were sufficiently important that the world should hear of them?

Perhaps the events were remarkable enough in themselves. Certainly this would be the case with an event such as the resurrection, which could not be ignored and which forces a re-evaluation of Jesus' identity.[37] But, as remarkable as the events were, they were not left as raw data. These events gained their great significance through being explained in connection with God's great plans for the world. The early apostolic preaching, then the teaching of the apostle Paul and eventually that of the Gospels, explained Jesus against the expectations generated by Israel's Scriptures, by prophecy, pattern and history. That is, the events reported by the Gospels were understood as events

[36] I. Levinskaya, *The Book of Acts in its First Century Setting*. Vol. 5: *Diaspora Setting* (Carlisle and Grand Rapids: Paternoster & Eerdmans, 1996), chs. 1–2. See also S. J. D. Cohen, 'Adolph Harnack's "The Mission and Expansion of Judaism": Christianity Succeeds Where Judaism Fails', in B. A. Pearson, A. T. Kraabel, G. W. E. Nickelsburg and N. R. Peterson, eds, *The Future of Christianity: Essays in Honor of Helmut Koester* (Minneapolis: Fortress, 1991) 163–197; M. Goodman, *Mission and Conversion. Proselytizing in the Religious History of the Roman Empire* (Oxford: Clarendon, 1994); S. McKnight, *A Light Among the Gentiles: Jewish Missionary Activity in the Second Temple Period* (Minneapolis: Fortress, 1991). For a critique of the new consensus, see L. H. Feldmann, *Jew and Gentile in the Ancient World. Attitudes and Interactions from Alexander to Justinian* (Princeton: Princeton University Press, 1993), Ch. 9; and J. C. Paget, 'Jewish Proselytism at the Time of Christian Origins: Chimera or Reality?', *JSNT* 62 (1996) 65–103.

[37] Cf N. T. Wright, 'Christian Origins and the Resurrection of Jesus: The Resurrection of Jesus as a Historical Problem', *Sewanee Theological Review* 41/2 (1998) 107–123.

with great *theological* significance. When understood against the theological framework erected by the OT Scriptures, the man from Nazareth was recognised to be someone of significance not only for Israel but also for all people. Christology gave birth to mission.

Theological framework of mission

According to the Scriptures

The Gospels show that John the Baptist spoke of Jesus as 'the coming one' (Matt 11:3 = Luke 7:19; cf Mark 1:7 = Matt 3:11 = Luke 3:16), and that Jesus himself had a clear sense of being sent by God for a particular purpose (Matt 15:24; 21:37; Luke 4:18; John 3:17; 3:34; 4:38).[38] Each of the Synoptic Gospels shows Jesus referring to God as 'the one who sent me' (Mark 9:37; Matt 10:40; Luke 9:48; 10:16), and in John's Gospel this is Jesus' constant practice (John 5:36; 6:29; 7:29; 10:36; 17:3,18; 20:21). This awareness is entirely suitable for any prophet who has been sent on a mission from God, such as the OT prophets (cf Mark 12:1–12; Luke 13:34), or John the Baptist (Mark 1:2; Luke 7:27; John 1:6; 3:28), but Jesus was also aware that he came in contradistinction to the other prophets, for he came as the one for whom they prepared the way.[39]

One of the burdens of the Gospel writers is to show how Jesus must be understood 'according to the Scriptures'. Although this is done in different ways by the four evangelists, each of them clearly feels that it was a task which they needed to do. The evidence we have from elsewhere (e.g. the early preaching in Acts, or the book of Romans), shows that this task formed the staple diet of the early Christian mission out of which the Gospels arose. The events of Jesus Christ were proclaimed as events which fulfilled the Scriptures.

---

[38] This awareness came from a two-fold source: (1) the sustained study of the Scriptures from an early age, in which Jesus showed exceptional facility (cf Luke 2:41–52); (2) God's announcement at Jesus' baptism designated him as the one to whom the Scriptures were pointing, and from then on, his mission was launched.

[39] Cf. Mark 12:1–12, where the son is the last in a succession of prophets.

In this task, the covenantal framework of the OT, beginning with the promises to Abraham, was important, especially for the theme of mission, since Abraham was promised that all the families of the earth would be blessed through him (Gen 12:1–3). These promises to Abraham are important to the structure of the OT, including the later prophets. They are alluded to by Matthew (1:1, 2, 17; 3:9; 8:11; 22:32) and John (8:31–58), and explicitly quoted by Luke–Acts in the portrayal of the gospel mission spreading out to the ends of the earth (Luke 1:55, 73; 3:8, 34; 13:16, 28; 16:22–30; 19:9; 20:37; Acts 3:13, 25; 7:2, 16, 17, 32; 13:26).[40]

But this general biblical theological framework is focused through certain specific texts, to which the Gospels refer over and again as being of crucial importance for understanding who Jesus really was. The OT had generated expectations about the one who was to come, and Jesus was explained in the light of these key texts. He was the Christ, the Suffering Servant, the Lord, and the Son of Man who exercises supreme authority in the Kingdom of God.

As soon as Jesus is identified in terms of these OT expectations, his role is also defined. These texts do not merely explain who Jesus is, but they also explain what Jesus did. These texts provide the theological framework within which Jesus operated, and, at the same time as they explain his true identity, they explain his mission.

The Christ (Psalm 2)

This Psalm lies behind Jesus' designation as the Son of God. The Son of God in Psalm 2 was God's anointed king, ruling in Zion. The nations rage against him, but God issues them a warning to kiss the feet of the Son, or suffer his wrath.

In the synoptic Gospel, the voice from heaven at Jesus' baptism and his transfiguration cites Psalm 2:7: 'You are my Son' (Mark 1:11; 9:7; Matt 3:17; 17:5; Luke 3:22; 9:35). The title Son of God clearly plays a key role in their presentation of Jesus, and perhaps even more so in John's Gospel.

---

40 Barrett, 'Gentile Mission', 73, argues that the promise to Abraham determines the Gentile mission as the second stage after that to the Jews.

For our purposes, Luke uses the Psalm in a particularly interesting way in Acts 4. Matthew and Mark present Jesus' crucifixion as being the moment when Jesus was handed over to the Gentiles (Mark 10:33; Matt 20:19). John echoes the same notion by presenting Pilate's words at Jesus' trial: 'Am I a Jew? Your nation and your High Priest handed you over to me!' (John 18:35). Luke's Gospel repeats the same idea (Luke 18:32), and in his second volume, Luke shows that this aspect of the crucifixion fulfils Psalm 2 (Acts 4:25–28). But the Psalm and its fulfilment are quoted in the context of a prayer for boldness to preach the gospel (vv 29–30) in the face of continued opposition by those who had conspired against Jesus. Perhaps Psalm 2 also lies behind this prayer, for in the Psalm God had promised the Son 'ask of me and I will make the nations your heritage and the ends of the earth your possession' (Ps 2:8). As their request is granted (v 31), the gospel is boldly proclaimed and so the nations continue to be given to the Son as it advances towards the ends of the earth (cf. Acts 1:8). Thus, the identity of Jesus as Son of God, implies that the nations will be his.

The Suffering Servant (Isaiah)

The 'suffering servant' is the major figure in Isaiah's 'book of comfort' (Isa 40–55).[41] This prophetic-kingly figure is to bring salvation to the people of Israel languishing under the Lord's judgment. He is related to the arrival of the news of forgiveness of their sins, and the promise of a new start (Isa 40:1, 2). Strangely, this is achieved through the suffering and death of the Servant himself. Since the Servant was prepared to die, the Lord promised to raise him up in glory (53:10–12).

The salvation achieved by this Servant of the Lord was going to be so marvellous, it would not be enough to achieve the salvation of Israel alone (Isa 49:1–5). The Servant is therefore equipped with God's Spirit to bring justice to the nations (Isa 42:1,4); he will be a light to the nations bringing salvation to the ends of the earth (49:6); and even in his death Gentile kings will shut their mouths because of what he achieves on their behalf (52:15; 53:4–6).

---

[41] Cf. W. J. Dumbrell, 'The Role of the Servant in Isaiah 40–55', *RTR* 48 (1989) 105–113.

The presentation of Jesus as the Servant of the Lord is a major part of the Christology of the synoptic Gospels. It also lies behind John's insistence that the good shepherd will lay down his life for the sheep (John 10) and especially behind the statement that Jesus is raised up because he willingly lays down his life in this way (John 10:18, contrast 19:10–11; cf. Isa 53:10–12). Jesus willingly dies as the servant 'who gives his life as a ransom for many' (Mark 10:45; Matt 20:28; cf Luke 22:37), and so he is vindicated by the Lord.

It must be stressed that as soon as Jesus adopted the role of the Servant of the Lord (ie at his baptism when the Spirit anointed him), salvation to the nations was in view. What occurred through his death on the cross was too big for Israel alone. It is no surprise, therefore, when the book of Acts shows the Servant passages still playing a determinative role as the gospel spreads further amongst the nations (e.g. Acts 3:13, 26; 13:47).

David's Lord (Psalm 110)

Each of the Synoptics report Jesus in controversy with his opponents on a number of occasions. When they had finally had enough of trying to trap him through debate and tricky questions, Jesus turned the tables on them by questioning their Christology. He did this through Psalm 110:1. How can the Messiah be the son of David, if David calls him Lord? (Mark 12:35–37; Matt 22:41–45; Luke 20:41–44; cf John 7:42). Although this Psalm is not cited frequently, its importance comes from being cited at a key narrative position at the end of Jesus' public confrontation with the leaders of Israel and before they get him out of the way secretly through the betrayal of Judas. At his trial, Jesus also cites this Psalm, indicating that it will be fulfilled after he rises from the dead to 'sit at God's right hand' (Mark 14:62; Matt 26:64; Luke 22:69).

The designation of Jesus by Psalm 110:1 has implications for his mission. The fulfilment of this Psalm in the exaltation of Jesus launches the gospel mission on the day of Pentecost (Acts 2:34–36). Why? Because the exaltation of the Messiah to the position of Lord at God's right hand was so that the conquest of his enemies might begin. Although Jesus was crucified by human beings, the Lord has declared his verdict by raising him, and sitting him at his right hand 'until I make your enemies a footstool'. Thus, from the moment of the resurrection God is placing the enemies of Jesus under his feet, and this is occurring through the proclamation of the gospel and will not be completed until the final day (cf. 1 Cor 15:20–28). In Jesus' heavenly session, he presides over his work of mission.

The Son of Man and the kingdom of God (Daniel)

At the peak of the Gospels' Christology is the portrayal of Jesus in terms of Daniel's Son of Man. In Daniel's vision in chapter 7, after seeing the human kingdoms of the world pictured as devouring beasts, spreading destruction and death, Daniel sees a judgment scene and one like a Son of Man coming to the ancient days to receive the kingdom. Previously Daniel had spoken of the kingdom of God being set up as a replacement to all human kingdoms, one which will never be destroyed (2:44); now this kingdom of God is given to the Son of Man at the throne of the ancient of days (7:13–14). This means that the expectation of the arrival of the kingdom of God is bound up with the coming of the Son of Man.

In the Gospels, Jesus' preference for this title as his self-designation is well-known, and, as can be expected from the book of Daniel, it is frequently associated with the coming kingdom of God. The powerful implications of this title have often been missed, however, through an interpretation which is erroneous.[42] When the synoptic Gospels refer to the coming of the Son of Man, this has often been taken to refer to Jesus' second coming (ie a coming to earth at the end of time). It should be taken in the same sense as its original quotation, namely, to refer to the coming of the Son of Man to God in his resurrection/exaltation, which is when he was awarded supreme position in the kingdom of God. That this understanding is correct is confirmed by its combination with Ps 110:1 in the Synoptic Gospels' account of the trial (Mark 14:62; Matt 26:64; Luke 22:69); by the

---

[42] I have explored this further in 'The Narrative Integrity of Mark 13:24–27', (Unpublished MTh thesis; Australian College of Theology, 1991), the argument of which is now summarised in 'Mark 13: An Apocalyptic Precursor to the Passion Narrative' *RTR* 54 (1995) 10–32.

Gospel of John, where the Son of Man is frequently referred to as being 'lifted up' in the exaltation; and by the book of Acts where the title is used of the exalted Christ (Acts 7:55, with an allusion to Ps 110:1) and the second coming is referred to in entirely different language.

Jesus' designation as the Son of Man has very important implications for the gospel mission. In Jesus' apocalyptic discourse, just before he went to his own death, he attempted to re-set his disciples' expectations so that they would begin to look for the 'coming of the Son of Man' (Mark 13:24–26). In doing so, he stated that when the Son of Man comes, to receive the kingdom of God from the hands of the Ancient of Days, he would then send out his messengers to gather in the elect from the four corners of the earth (Mark 13:27). This indicates that the great time of harvest begins with Jesus' resurrection and exaltation to heaven, and that this harvest is actually performed by the glorified Son of Man through his chosen messengers. This provides a very powerful underpinning to the work of mission, which, is apparent in the other Gospels too, as well as in the book of Acts.

So the Gospels are about certain key events which occurred in the real world, but they explain those events in terms of the fulfilment of the theological expectations erected by the OT. In doing so, they provide a theological understanding of Jesus which also provides a theological rationale for mission. They also set him in a particular eschatological framework. For with his arrival 'the times are fulfilled' (Mark 1:15) and, since his resurrection/exaltation begins 'the last days' (Acts 2:16–17), the gospel mission also takes on a note of eschatological urgency.[43]

The final thing to observe in this section is that the Gospels are persuasive documents, in that they seek to join people to Jesus' mission. But this persuasion is by means of a narrative. The Gospels seek to graft people into Jesus' mission, through presenting the theologically significant events of Jesus Christ in narrative form.

---

[43] For the importance of eschatology and mission see: O. Cullmann, 'Eschatology and Missions in the New Testament', in G. H. Anderson, ed., *The Theology of the Christian Mission* (London: SCM, 1961) 42–54; J. A. Scherer, 'Why Mission Theology Cannot Do Without Eschatological Urgency. The Significance of the End', *Missiology* 18/4 (1990) 405–413, and Scherer, 'Mission Theology', 199.

Persuasion through narrative

As with any portion of Scripture, the danger of a moralistic reading of the Gospels needs to be avoided. The Bible reading methods of popular piety which encourage the quest for 'a command to follow', 'a promise to cling onto', or 'an example to avoid or to follow' may not be of much help in reading the Gospel narratives, and this may partly explain why the Gospels are avoided more often than they ought to be. The epistles provide a much better source from which to mine nuggets which promise changed Christian behaviour.

Such an approach also needs to be avoided in our quest for the foundations of mission. I have already alluded to such an approach, in which it is claimed that the NT contains a paucity of commands motivating Christian people towards evangelistic mission. This assumes that Christian motivation comes from a moralistic framework, that is, there is a command, so we obey it. It is a pity that the obvious shallowness of this exegetical method for constructing the Christian life, not to mention its complete barrenness for constructing any kind of coherent Christian theology, is not as obvious as it should be, for it keeps on doing the rounds.

Moralistic interpretations of the Bible are not only the domain of the ordinary Bible reader, they are also perpetuated at a more scholarly level. In the Gospels, for example, there is a tendency to be overly interested in the disciples as models (or otherwise) of behaviour. Certainly there is some truth to this, but there is much more to be said. Narratives work with a far greater complexity than a moralistic framework allows. A narrative offers an entire web of relationships amongst characters both positive and negative, a developing story, a time frame, a set of geographical relationships, emotions, dialogue, scenes and summaries, a beginning, middle and end that makes contact with its reader through all these means and in a variety of ways. The narrative engages the reader's mind, body and soul, and through the entire complex process we know as 'reading', seeks to move the reader in a certain direction.

It is my conviction that the Gospel narratives present the events of Jesus' ministry, death and resurrection as theologically significant events, and that through all the complexities of their narratives, seek to persuade readers to join the mission of Jesus.[44]

Part B will consist of a cursory look at this process through examining some key sections from each of the Gospels.

Mission in the Gospels

What was Jesus' mission? How were the first apostles related to his mission? How are we related to their mission and so to Jesus' mission?

Mark

(1) Jesus' mission

As the Servant of the Lord, Jesus came to an Israel that was in great need. Israel was smitten by unclean spirits and various diseases which, according to the OT picture, should never have been suffered by God's people. The prophet Isaiah had pictured Israel's terrible situation using sickness metaphors: the people were blind, they were deaf, they needed healing. But this situation was caused by their sin and God's answering judgment. Israel lived under the shadow of death, because they had deserted their God. They needed forgiveness, they needed salvation.[45]

Jesus served Israel as the Servant of the Lord, healing their illnesses as a picture of forgiveness (Mark 2:10,17), casting out the unclean spirits, just like the prophet Zechariah had promised (Zech 13:2), and eventually dying as a ransom for many (Mark 10:45) to bring forgiveness, salvation, entry into eternal life. He preached the message of the kingdom, despite Israel's hardness

---

44 I have explored some of the narrative dynamics used by Mark in 'What is the Gospel for Today's Church?', in B. G. Webb, ed., *Exploring The Missionary Church* (Homebush West, NSW: ANZEA, 1993), 27–59; and in ' "Do You Not Care That We Are Perishing?" Jesus' Defeat of Death and Mark's Early Readers' (Unpublished PhD thesis, King's College London, 1997).

45 For this paragraph, see P. G. Bolt, ' ". . . With a View to the Forgiveness of Sins": Jesus and forgiveness in Mark's Gospel', *RTR* 57/2 (1998) 53–69.

of heart (4:10–11). As he preached the word, a remnant from within Israel were raised up (4:3–6, 12–20, cf Isa 6:11). These were the ones who would be sent out as workers into the harvest.

Jesus also spoke of the time when the harvest would extend beyond the borders of Israel. In his apocalyptic discourse, he spoke of the gospel going to the nations as such a priority that its preachers ought to be prepared to suffer for it (13:10). He was Daniel's Son of Man, and when the Son of Man comes to the Father to receive the kingdom, then he will send his messengers out to the nations to gather together the elect from the ends of the earth (13:24–27).

(2) . . . and the Twelve

The twelve are gathered together to assist him in his mission to Israel. When Jesus calls the first disciples, he uses an image of judgment when he promises he will make them fish for people (Mark 1:16–20; cf Jer 16:16). As they function in this role, they will bring judgment through separation of one person from another, bringing division to the heart of Israel (13:12–13; cf Mic 7:6).

In response to the pressure of people coming from all quarters (3:7-13), Jesus called twelve together as a group, which Mark identifies (3:14–19). He called them for two reasons: that they might be with him and that they might be sent out to preach and to have authority over the *daimons*. Since these activities mirror exactly those Jesus had been engaged in, the disciples are portrayed as extending his ministry. Their ministry will be exercised in the same manner as that of Jesus, with preaching of the kingdom as the primary activity, with the cleansing of the land of Israel from unclean spirits consequent upon it (cf 1:22–28).

This picture is confirmed when Mark tells of the disciples being sent out (6:7–13). They are granted authority over the spirits (6:7), but when they go out they act as messengers (6:11) who preach repentance (6:12), with the accompaniment of healing and exorcism. When King Herod hears of what they are doing, their ministry raises questions about who Jesus is (6:14–16), which indicates that the twelve were an extension of Jesus' ministry to Israel. The number 'twelve' is symbolic of the tribes of Israel and is important in Jewish eschatological expectation. The Gospel of Mark pictures Jesus calling the twelve to assist him in his task of gathering a remnant from Israel before the last day arrives.

The twelve are also the 'messengers' who will be sent out into the harvest of all the earth following the exaltation of the Son of Man (13:24–27). Although their training process is long and difficult, and not without its failures, as he goes to his death Jesus promises them that, despite them falling away, he will gather them together in Galilee after he has risen (14:27–28). In fulfilment of this prediction, the young man in white at the empty tomb asks the women to tell his disciples to meet him in Galilee (16:7). Although Mark closes his story without reporting the results of this meeting, it is generally taken as the moment when the disciples were launched into the harvest of the Gentiles.[46]

(3) . . . and others

But what of other followers of Jesus, besides the twelve? In Mark's Gospel no-one else is commissioned to share in Jesus' mission, either to Israel before his passion, or to the nations beyond his resurrection.

However, other people are called to respond positively to Jesus. On two occasions he speaks generally about what is involved for anyone who follows him (Mark 8:34–9:1; 10:28–31). For the sake of entering the kingdom to inherit eternal life, Jesus asks for a radical discipleship which requires the renunciation of all of the structures of human life which normally provide security and demand loyalty. It is interesting that he demands a loyalty both to him, and to his mission, for he asks for such radical choices to be made 'for my sake, and for the sake of the gospel/my words' (Mark 8:35, 38; 10:29). Normal discipleship is radical, and it means being thoroughly committed to his mission in a hostile world.

Notice that this group are still not the twelve. They follow like the twelve. They are to give the same radical loyalty to Jesus' mission as the twelve, and they receive the same promises as the twelve. And yet, they are not the twelve. They do not receive the

---

[46] I take it that 16:8 is Mark's original and intended ending.

same commission as the twelve. Whereas the twelve were commissioned with full authority to preach as an extension of Jesus' own ministry, the call for the others is that they might be 'unashamed' of the gospel. This still entails speaking the gospel, but it is on a different level to the direct commissioning the twelve received from their master to act as an extension of his own ministry.

(4) . . . and still more others

Mark also shows many others responding to Jesus, namely, those who were healed by him in some way. The usual response of these people is to begin to speak about what Jesus has done for them. Even if Jesus had told them not to, they could not contain themselves from speaking about how the Lord had mercy upon them (cf. Mark 1:45; 5:19–20; 7:36). If the twelve are the fishermen, these people represent the fish. When they were healed, they did not heal in return, but they spoke about what had occurred when they met Jesus. They were unashamed of Jesus' mission, because Jesus had brought them salvation and they began to live again; so they spoke of him.

These people are the bridge to the readers of the Gospel.[47] Are the readers of the Gospel to be engaged in the harvest of the nations? Yes they are, because they are the nations being harvested. As the Gospel is read, they too are called to respond to who Jesus is and what he has done on their behalf in his death and resurrection. They too are to follow him radically, for the sake of entering the kingdom. They too are to be unashamed of him or of his mission, and they too will speak of the one who has brought them salvation and life.

The readers of the Gospel are not the twelve. They are part of the nations, to whom the Son of Man sent his messengers to reap a harvest. They are that harvest, and the twelve are the ones through whom they have been reaped. Through its connection with the twelve, Mark's Gospel is like the sickle that has been thrust into the harvest field: through this story of Jesus, the readers come to know the gospel which the messengers have proclaimed to the nations. The twelve form a bridge

---

[47] Cf. Bolt, 'Jesus' Defeat'.

between the readers of the Gospel and the one who is met within its pages.

Since the other Synoptics follow roughly the same pattern, I will focus upon their distinctive endings, which simply enhance and clarify the picture already presented by Mark.

Matthew's great commission

(1) The climax of Jesus' mission

The final scene in Matthew's Gospel is the climax of Jesus' mission. Jesus has exercised his ministry to Israel, raising up a remnant and exercising judgment by creating a division amongst the people. He has sent out the twelve on a mission which he had explicitly restricted to Israel, forbidding them to go to the nations (Matt 10).

However, from the beginning of the Gospel, the nations have been on view. Matthew's genealogy linked Jesus with Abraham, and contained four Gentile women; the kings from the east (Matthew 2) represent the Gentile nations who were meant to stream into Zion in the last days (eg Isa 2:1–4). When Jesus gathered together his remnant, he did so by reference to 'the city on the hill' (Matt 5:13), another allusion to the mountain of the Lord to which the Gentiles would stream in the last days. Matthew referred to Jesus as the Servant of the Lord and inserted a long quotation at a key point in the narrative which spoke of him not giving up 'until he brings justice to the Gentiles, and until the Gentiles hope in his name' (12:18–21).

Even before Jesus had begun his ministry proper, Matthew had explained his move to live in Capernaum in terms of its proximity to the Gentiles, for, he explained, this move fulfilled the prophet Isaiah's words that the people who sit in darkness and the shadow of death will see a great light (Matt 4:12–17, cf Isa 9:2).

The Great Commission is delivered once again in this region, Galilee of the Gentiles (Matt 28:16), so the story of Jesus has come full circle. Jesus announces to the Eleven, that all authority on heaven and earth has been given to him. Now that he has risen from the dead, he has been installed as the Son of

Man.[48] The kingdom of God is now his; no human authority exists apart from his own. As the logical outcome of this authority being given to him, he launches the mission to the nations (Matt 28:19).

(2) The Gospel to the nations

The only command is 'to make disciples'. 'Go' is simply an auxiliary with little force, and the other two participles (baptising, teaching) show how the disciples are to be made.

Who are the nations? Although some have argued for an understanding of 'the nations' as being inclusive of Israel, I prefer to see 'the nations' as the Gentiles.[49] The phrase has this meaning in Isaiah, which informs Matthew's usage (eg Matt 12:18–21, cf. Isa 42:1–4). Even though Matthew uses the expression 'all the nations', rather than simply 'the nations', the two expressions are synonymous.

Jesus is launching a new stage of his mission, and this is the counterpart to the mission to Israel in chapter 10. Then the disciples were sent on a mission which they would not complete before the Son of Man came (Matt 10:23); now the Son of Man has come, and the nations are to be harvested as well.

(3) Whose commission?

The commission is addressed to the eleven (Matt 28:16), but does it apply to anyone else? The Reformers said it was to the eleven alone. William Carey extended it to all believers everywhere, as long as the end of the age had not arrived.[50] So who is involved in this mission to the nations?

An answer emerges along the same lines proposed for the Markan material. The commission is given to the eleven disciples, who are the special group chosen by Jesus. They are

---

[48] K. Barth, 'An Exegetical Study of Matthew 28:16–20', in Anderson, *Theology*, 61.

[49] The possiblilities are discussed in O'Brien, 'Great Commission', 73–75. Barth, 'Study', 64, points out that although the sending is to the nations, this does not exclude Israel from mission; 'Her right of the first-born, her *dignitas primogenitureae*, as Calvin called it, remains unimpaired. Yet the disciples are summoned to go out to the Gentile people and nations.'

[50] Bosch, 'Reflections', 176.

the ones who receive the commission as such. They are to make disciples through teaching them what Jesus had taught them first. There is another group mentioned in the Great Commission: those who are made disciples by the apostles' teaching. The readers of the Gospel would naturally associate themselves with this group. Once again, the apostles' specialness ought to be preserved. They are the ones who take the gospel to the nations. It is through their word that the teaching of Jesus is made known to the world, and through that teaching others become disciples. Those who are made disciples may well teach the things of Jesus as well, and others will be made disciples through the process, but they will teach the things of Jesus by teaching the apostolic words. For it is in the apostles' written words that we now find the words of Jesus. Jesus' word does not come to us in an unmediated form, it comes to us through the words of that first group of specially commissioned apostles. This is even clearer in Luke's writings.[51]

Luke

(1) Early days

The Gentiles are on view from the beginning of Luke's Gospel and from the early days of Jesus' ministry, even though Luke also reports that his ministry was focused upon Israel. Jesus sends out the twelve, and he also sends out the seventy as part of the mission to Israel. This brings judgment on Israel through division and a remnant is raised up. But for the most part Israel doesn't recognise this time of visitation when the Kingdom of God drew near in the person of Jesus (Lk. 19:44). In the final chapter of the Gospel, Jesus launches his mission to the nations.

(2) Jesus' mission to the nations (Luke 24)

After the resurrection, Jesus appears to the two disciples walking to Emmaus. Their hopes for Jesus redeeming Israel had

[51] Further to what follows, see Bolt, 'Mission and Witness'. Barrett, 'Gentile Mission', 71, points out that the mission to the Gentiles is one of Luke's keenest interests.

been dashed by his crucifixion (24:21), but Jesus explains from the Scriptures that these things had to occur (24:25–27): the Christ had to suffer and then enter his glory. When he appears to the rest of the disciples, he also explains the recent events in the light of the Scriptures, explaining that three things had to happen, because they were part of God's plan (24:45). First, the Messiah had to suffer; second, he had to rise from the dead; and third, repentance and the forgiveness of sins were to be proclaimed to all nations, beginning from Jerusalem. At this point in Luke's story, two out of three of these Scriptural necessities had already occurred. The only thing left to be completed was the proclamation of repentance and forgiveness of sins to the nations. Jesus articulates that, in God's plans, as revealed by God's word, the purpose of the times beyond the resurrection is the mission to the nations. He then commissions the disciples to be his specially appointed witnesses to these things.

(3) The continued witness of the witnesses (Acts)

The book of Acts shows these witnesses going about their task of testifying to the risen Jesus and preaching the forgiveness of sins. Through their ministry, the mission of Jesus continues, and they repeatedly refer to these three Scriptural necessities.

As the story continues, Paul is also commissioned as a witness, specially chosen to testify to the nations and he too is aware of the three Scriptural necessities. Towards the end of Acts (26:15–23), one of Paul's speeches forms a suitable summary of the theological underpinning for the mission that has been described across the course of the book:

> I stand here, testifying to both small and great, saying nothing but what the prophets and Moses said would take place: that the Messiah must suffer, and that, by being the first to rise from the dead, he would proclaim light both to our people [=Israel] and to the Gentiles. (Acts 26:22,23)

Clearly there are three crucial stages to God's plans, and the time in which Paul preached, and in which we still live, is the time for the proclamation of light to the nations.

It is even clearer in Luke that those from the nations who believe are not the ones who have been specially commissioned to be the witnesses. This group were witnesses of the resurrection, and in order to do this they had to have been with Jesus from the beginning (Acts 1:21–22; 2:32; 10:40–41).

Those who converted to Christ spoke a lot about Christ and praised God for what had occurred, but this did not elevate them to become the specially appointed witnesses to Christ. Since Acts keeps on providing the words of the witnesses in their many speeches, a good case can be mounted that Luke does this in order that the witness of the witnesses can continue whenever Acts is read. In other words, the readers of Luke–Acts are linked to the events of Jesus Christ through the apostolic word, through the narrative of Luke–Acts. Jesus sent his witnesses to us, in his kindness, and their witness is now enshrined in what has been written. We participate in Jesus' mission through their word, and we participate in it by receiving the word of salvation. In response, we most certainly share that message with others, for our response will certainly be verbal, as we praise God for what he has done in Christ. But we do not have the same commission as the apostles and we cannot ever assume their role. They continue to exercise their mission whenever their word is read. When we speak, we simply point back to the apostolic word. We tell their stories over and over again.

John

(1) The Son of Man's lifting up

John's Gospel strains ahead to 'the hour' when the Son of Man is lifted up in the exaltation (2:4; 4:21, 23; 5:25, 28, 7:30; 8:20; 12:23, 27; 13:1; 17:1). The Son of Man is exalted because, like the Servant of the Lord, he was prepared to willingly lay down his life for the sheep (10:17–18). As the Good Shepherd he knew that he had 'other sheep that were not of this fold', those who were not of Israel, and he laid down his life, so that this flock of God might be gathered together, as 'one flock, under one shepherd' (10:16). Thus the aim of Jesus' death and resurrection is to gather together the flock of God. Ultimately the goal is to raise this flock at the last day and give them eternal life (10:28–29; cf. 6:39, 44).

In an ironic twist, Caiaphas is shown to prophesy about the same thing. When he states that Jesus ought to die for the nation, John declares this a prophecy 'that Jesus was about to die for the nation'. He then adds, 'and not for the nation only, but to gather into one the dispersed children of God' (John 11:51–52).

The climax of the first half of the Gospel comes in John 12, where Jesus' enemies declare that 'the world has gone after him' (John 12:19). When some Greeks come to Jesus he takes it as a signal that his hour has come; it is time for the glorification of the Son of Man (12:20–23). He then speaks metaphorically, saying that a grain of wheat must die in order for it to bear much fruit (12:24). Shortly after, the meaning of the metaphor becomes apparent, when he declares that 'when I am lifted up from the earth, I will draw all people to myself' (12:31). John explains that he said this about the kind of death he was going to die. Jesus was going to die a death which would lead to him being lifted up so that he might draw all people to himself.[52]

Here, before the passion is recounted, John provides his readers with an explanation of Jesus' death in terms of mission. Jesus was sent to do the Father's will, and this was to raise up his people at the last day; to unite the flock of God which are now scattered throughout the world under the one shepherd. This would be achieved through the Son of Man being lifted up and drawing all people to himself.

(2) The sending of the Twelve

Even though Jesus' disciples bring people to him at several points (1:45; 12:20,21), John never records them being sent out on a mission to Israel. When they are in Samaria, however, Jesus tells them that there is a harvest ripe for the taking and that they have been given the privilege of reaping where another has sown (4:35–38). Interestingly enough, when the Samaritans believe, it is in recognition, even at this stage in the story, that Jesus is the Saviour not of Israel, but of the world (4:42).

Once the first half of the Gospel reaches its climax in chapter 12, and the expectation is erected that Jesus would draw all

---

[52] I have argued this case in 'What Fruit Does the Vine Bear? Some Pastoral Implications of John 15:1–8', *RTR* 51 (1992) 11–19.

people to himself, bearing much fruit, Jesus begins to train his disciples for their special role in this world harvest (13–17). He would send them the Spirit to help them recall his words, and to convict the world of sin, righteousness and judgment. Although more could be said, here we see Jesus preparing his apostles to be the writers of the NT, which allows for the future in which the Spirit and the apostles work together to bear fruit in the world.

(3) . . . to the others

Jesus' high priestly prayer shows this 'chain of command' from Jesus to the apostles (17:6–19), to the others who believe through their word (17:20). In the same way that the Father sent the Son, Jesus sends the apostles into the world (17:18; cf. 20:21), so that they might bring his word to the world, resulting in 'oneness' (17:21), that the one flock under one shepherd might be brought together. There are clearly three levels in this mission of the Son: he does the sending; the apostles are sent with his word; and others believe in Jesus Christ through the apostles' word.

After the farewell discourses are over, Jesus is crucified, then rises, and in John 21 the disciples' mission is launched, when Jesus tells Peter to tend his lambs. 'Bring together the flock of God!'

Once again, the same things can be said as for the Synoptics. The readers of John's Gospel are joined to Jesus' mission through the mission of the apostles. Eternal life comes to those who believe their word, for that is how Jesus' word is mediated to the world. Jesus' death bears much fruit in the world, as the apostles preach his word and people come to believe in Jesus through them (17:20). This group of men had a special, historic, unrepeatable role. They were sent on a special mission from Jesus. Their mission continues in the pages of the NT. As we read the Gospels, we are connected with the apostolic mission, and through them with Jesus' mission.

Do we have a mission too? We too will see people converted through the word of Jesus. As we abide in Jesus' word through them, so the vine bears much fruit (15:5,8). The fruitfulness of the vine occurs as the individual branches abide in the vine. They abide as they hear, believe and obey Jesus' word as proclaimed by the apostles.

Following Jesus and Fishing for People

Foundations of Mission

(1) Historical foundation

What foundations have we discovered for the work of mission in the third millennium? We have our roots in the new and aggressively missionary movement which sprang up after Jesus of Nazareth rose from the dead. Since the Gospels sprang out of that mission in order to support that mission, they provide a window into the reasons why earliest Christianity had this missionary nature. When these reasons are examined, it becomes apparent that far from being historically specific, they provide justification for the Jesus' movement to maintain its missionary character throughout the millennia.

(2) Christological foundation

Jesus was regarded as the fulfilment of OT expectation. The expectations erected by the OT were used to explain who he was and what he did. He was sent to die, and to rise again to save, to bring forgiveness of sins, eternal life and entry to the kingdom of God. An understanding of Jesus' mission shows that mission is evangelistic at its core; 'love' is the ethos, but salvation for the age to come through the forgiveness of sins is the goal.

(3) Theological foundation

The Father sent the Son, so Jesus' mission arises from God's mission. God is glorified through the work that Jesus did. Jesus came as the climax of God's plan of salvation. Evangelistic mission springs from the heart of God, and so should be at the heart of all else in his world and in his church. It should therefore encompass all else. All else we do as a church or as individuals ought to be done with reference to God's plan to save in Jesus Christ.

(4) Eschatological foundation

Jesus came as the fulfilment of God's plans, as the fulfilment of OT eschatological expectation. His death and resurrection were two of the final three 'events' in God's plan. In God's plan, the times since the resurrection are the last days. The purpose of the times is the proclamation of forgiveness of sins to the nations.

Evangelistic mission must go on and takes priority over all else. It is both urgent and important, for it is the divine priority for the times in which we live. This priority should help churches and individuals to order their activities.

(5) Apostolic foundation

The risen Jesus continues his mission by sending his chosen witnesses on their mission to harvest the nations. These men cannot and should not be bypassed. The apostles form the link between Jesus and all who come after them. We are joined to the Son and so to the Father only through believing the apostles' word which was written under the superintendence of the Spirit.

So mission is not only evangelistic, it needs to be evangelical, firmly based on the apostolic gospel. They cannot be bypassed, because Jesus' mission is continued through them. The continued proclamation of their word is the means by which Jesus' mission continues across the millennia.

(6) Personal foundation

As we face the third millennium, the fields are still ripe for harvest and the last days' harvest has already begun. It began with the risen Jesus and continues wherever the apostolic word is proclaimed.

As the apostolic gospel comes to us, we are part of the harvest field. We are called upon to repent and believe the gospel of forgiveness. As we do so, there is a call to radical discipleship, a call to reorder all of our life according to gospel priorities, according to the harvest in which Christ has been engaged for centuries, and which is still going on all around us. There is a call for us to be unashamed of Jesus and his gospel, that is, of Jesus and his gospel mission. This call brings with it the great privilege of speaking about him to others, a speech which issues from the overflow of a heart set free (cf. Matt 12:34): 'We believe, therefore we speak' (cf. 2 Cor 4:13).

As we speak, we must speak the gospel of Jesus Christ brought to us by the apostles. As we speak that apostolic word,

Jesus' mission continues in these last times in which we live. We need to lift up our eyes and see that the fields are ripe for harvest and then pray that the Lord of the harvest sends out labourers into the field. The risen Jesus has been given the nations as an inheritance. As we believe, so we will speak.

Exploring further

1. If Christianity began as a missionary movement, can modern 'Christianity' fail to be missionary and still be Christianity?
2. How do the various foundations outlined above assist in deciding the nature of the Christian mission? (ie what should Christian missionaries be doing?)
3. What is the place of the exposition of the New Testament in Christian mission?
4. If mission is not simply one of many activities, but a super-ordinate goal, how do the foundations outlined above assist in ordering the priorities of a local church, of a Christian denomination, or of Christian individuals?
5. Pretend you are leading a 'missionary' church service. Construct some prayers that are informed by the Gospels' input on mission.
6. Pretend that you are a 'missionary' home on furlough and about to join the 'deputation circuit'. Outline a talk that would attempt to motivate the congregations for mission.

2

Paul, Pluralism and Preaching: A Study in 1 Corinthians

Perry Wiles

Synopsis

At the end of the 20th century we live in a pluralist society which calls into question the validity of preaching the Christian gospel and the exclusive claims of Christ. Recognising that Paul also ministered in a pluralist setting, and that this was perhaps nowhere more the case than at Corinth, this paper focuses on 1 Corinthians and seeks to examine Paul's response to the issues and challenges of pluralism, including preaching in a pluralist setting.

To this end, after a brief introduction to 1 Corinthians and the pluralism of Corinth, exegetical observations are made on selected key passages from the letter which reveal aspects of Paul's response to the pluralism which confronted him and the believers of Corinth. Having surveyed these passages, an endeavour is made to discern the theological shape of Paul's thinking and some of the implications there might be for us in our pluralist setting.

It is observed that Paul does not deny that spiritual realities may underlie pagan religion, but nevertheless he eschews syncretism and relativism. He has a robust monotheism, which nevertheless includes Jesus Christ within its orb. Jesus is the unique Lord who shares in the very deity of God. Paul's understanding of the gospel, including its foolishness, its universality and its exclusivity are also discussed. All this provides a firm theological foundation for Christian engagement with our society with the gospel of Jesus Christ.

The siren song of pluralism

> Must we not all accept that truth is larger, richer, and more complex than can be contained in any one religious or cultural tradition? Is it not more fitting that we adopt the attitude of a humble seeker after truth, keeping an open mind, ready to listen to all that comes from the varied religious experience of the human race? Is it not more honest as well as more humble to stop preaching and engage rather in dialogue, listening to the experience of others and offering our own, not to displace theirs but to enrich and be enriched by the sharing of religious experience? Only an open mind can hope to reach the truth, and dogma is the enemy of the open mind.[1]

So Lesslie Newbigin describes the Siren song of pluralism with its ever so reasonable and irenic call to dialogue and mutual enrichment. In a world traumatised by conflict, strife and bigotry, much of which is religious, the suggestion that the major religious traditions are all culturally and historically conditioned responses to the same ultimate Reality is very attractive. Indeed many today assume that there is something morally blameworthy about evangelism and mission, and find any claims to Christian exclusivism intolerant and offensive.

How as evangelical Christians shall we respond to this call to leave off our preaching and our dogmas? The evangelical reflex is to head back to the Scriptures, and to seek to discern there the mind and will of God. This paper is intended as part of that process. It will focus on Paul's first letter to the Corinthians and explore what this letter might have to say concerning the issues and challenges with which pluralism confronts us, particularly in relation to the preaching of the gospel. But before we move to 1 Corinthians we should clarify some terms, not the least of which is 'pluralism' itself.

1 L. Newbigin, *The Gospel in a Pluralist Society* (London: SPCK, 1989) 7.

Pluralism now and then

It has become a commonplace to say that we live in a pluralist society, but what do we mean by that statement, and is it a new phenomenon? Don Carson in his book *The Gagging of God*, identifies at least three ways in which the word 'pluralism' is used:[2]

1. It is used to refer to the objective phenomenon of the sheer diversity of race, culture, values, lifestyle, language and religion found in many nations. Australia, as a result of post-war migration policy and multi-cultural policy, is objectively a pluralist society in this sense. Carson terms this 'empirical pluralism'.
2. The second way of using the term Carson labels 'cherished pluralism', by which he means that this diversity and plurality are celebrated as things to be approved and cherished. Multiculturalism is pluralist in this sense, a celebration of diversity, rather than an attempt to integrate people into one uniform culture.
3. The third use of the term 'pluralism' Carson labels 'philosophical pluralism'. This could also be called 'ideological pluralism', and is an aspect of post-modernism. It is the belief not only that pluralism in the first two senses is to be encouraged and desired, but that any normative claims to truth are to be censured and disallowed as imperialist and divisive. The appeal that Newbigin describes in the quote above, for example, clearly arises from a form of ideological pluralism. This ideological pluralism is an almost inevitable outworking of the Enlightenment's dethronement of external authorities and the enthronement of autonomous human reason as the chief authority in human thinking and understanding. It was only a matter of time before migration and travel would bring radically different cultures, religions and ways of thinking into close contact in such a way as to make very clear that *your* autonomous human reason doesn't always see eye to eye with *mine*.

---

[2] D. A. Carson, *The Gagging of God: Christianity Confronts Pluralism* (Grand Rapids: Zondervan, 1996) 13–22.

The result? A clash of competing truth claims with no possibility of an umpire to blow the whistle, and consequently, the radical loss of confidence in human reason and its ability to discern any ultimate truth that is one of the marks of post-modernism. One reaction to this is a collapse into complete relativism, with syncretism and eclecticism the order of the day. Another reaction, not necessarily exclusive of the other, is the trend towards tribalism, the fracturing of society into sub-cultures. This ideological pluralism also is an increasingly common feature of Australian society.

The importance of distinguishing between these varieties of pluralism is to clarify the point that, while as Christians we may wish to take issue with ideological pluralism, we can nevertheless still be quite appreciative of the benefits of living in the multicultural society which Australia has become at the end of the 20th century.

As Christians in Australia, we now live and seek to preach the gospel of Christ in a pluralist setting, a very different context to that of only a few decades ago. But it is important to realise that the Christian proclamation has always taken place in a pluralist world, in competition with rival religious and intellectual convictions.

Some aspects of the pluralism we face are undoubtedly novel (the modern form of ideological pluralism, for example), but the earliest Christians also wrestled with pluralism, including a form of ideological pluralism. In their case the pluralism was engendered by the unifying of the Mediterranean world under the Greeks and then the Romans which brought different cultures and religions into contact through increasing trade, travel and migration. In terms of the religious options available there were the traditional pantheons of Greece and Rome, in which a syncretistic identification of their respective deities was common; there were the Egyptian deities; the mystery cults; local fertility cults; the emperor cult; the philosophical schools of Stoicism and Epicureanism, and so on. These religious options were generally not seen as mutually exclusive. Polytheism is particularly open to syncretism—when you have a pantheon of many gods, what's one more! So although the precise shape of the pluralism Christians faced varied from place to place, the general religious milieu was pluralist and relativistic, with few religions making exclusive claims.[3]

Therefore, while recognising that there may be differences between the pluralism we face in twentieth-century Australia and that which confronted Paul in his missionary journeys around the first-century Mediterranean world, we can nevertheless profit from seeing how Paul brought his theology and practice to bear on his pluralist context and the situation of the Corinthian church, and discern both principles and pragmatics that may guide us in our pluralist setting, not least with regard to the preaching of the gospel.[4]

Pluralism, preaching and 1 Corinthians

The congregation in Corinth was established by Paul during his so-called second missionary journey. His ministry in Corinth is recorded by Luke in Acts 18. Paul stayed in Corinth at least 18 months, and when he departed for Ephesus he left behind an apparently thriving church, made up principally of Gentiles.[5]

Sometime after Paul had left Corinth, certain problems arose within the church which Paul seeks to deal with by means of the

---

[3] For a detailed discussion of the religious pluralism of the Hellenistic world see H. Koester, *Introduction to the New Testament. Volume 1: History, Culture, and Religion of the Hellenistic Age*. Vol. 1 (New York: Walter de Gruyter, 1995). Also D. W. J. Gill, 'Behind the Classical Facade. Local Religions of the Roman Empire.' In *One God, One Lord. Christianity in a World of Religious Pluralism* (Eds., A. D. Clarke and B. W. Winter; Grand Rapids: Baker, 1992) 85–100.

[4] During this paper I refer to 'the gospel' and to 'preaching the gospel'. It will be important to be clear on what Paul meant by these terms. There is scholarly debate about whether the NT use of *euangelizō*\ and its cognates has a Hellenistic or Jewish OT provenance, the latter particularly related to its usage in the LXX of Isaiah. A false dichotomy is often drawn here. The word group must derive its basic *denotation* from its general usage in the Hellenistic world, but its distinctive *connotation* in Christian usage (and in particular Paul's usage) comes by way of its usage in the LXX, where it refers to the announcement of God's rule and the salvation for his people that accompanies God's rule. Given this background 'preaching the gospel' for Paul can therefore be defined as follows:

To proclaim the gospel, to evangelise, is to announce the arrival of the Kingdom of God in the life, death and resurrection of Jesus Christ, Israel's Messiah, thereby summoning all people to give their allegiance to him by calling on his name for salvation and submitting to him as Lord in repentance and faith.

[5] 1 Corinthians 6:9–11; 8:7; and 12:1–3 presuppose a largely Gentile audience.

letter we know as 1 Corinthians. Many of these problems in Corinth appear to have arisen out of a form of over-realised eschatology that fed arrogance and a destructive spiritual elitism. The immediate occasion for the letter was two-fold: firstly a personal report from 'Chloe's people' (1:11) about divisions and strife in the church, and secondly a letter from Corinth seeking the apostle's advice on certain matters (7:1; 8:1; 12:1).

Pluralism in Corinth

Corinth at the time of Paul was a Roman colony of about one hundred thousand inhabitants. It was a prosperous city with two ports, straddling as it did the isthmus that separates the Peloponnese from mainland Greece. Since its refounding by Julius Caesar in 44 BC, Corinth had experienced rapid growth and a great influx of people from East and West, with the accompanying cultural and ethnic diversity that would have entailed.

Corinth was also a religiously diverse city. Around AD 170, Pausanias, a traveller to Corinth and other Greek cities, wrote about the many temples of Corinth in his book *The Description of Greece* (a sort of Lonely Planet guide to ancient Greece). In his discussion of the multitude of Corinth's gods he made no negative comment. As most of Corinth's inhabitants would have done, he simply accepted the legitimacy of the religious pluralism that he described. He mentioned at least 26 sacred places in the city, many of them temples. As well as the well known temple to Aphrodite, there were temples to other major and minor gods of the Roman and Greek pantheons. From Pausanias and other sources we know Corinth's pluralism also encompassed a number of Egyptian deities, many of the mystery cults, at least one Jewish synagogue, as well as the imperial cult.[6]

It was to this multicultural and religiously pluralist city that Paul came around AD 50 to preach the gospel of Jesus Christ, and it was here that the church that he founded had to struggle with living as Christians in this pluralist setting.

[6] For a detailed discussion of the religious pluralism in 1st century Corinth see B. W. Winter, 'Theological and Ethical Responses to Religious Pluralism—1 Corinthians 8–10.' *Tyndale Bulletin* 41, no. 2 (1990) 209 226.

Exegetical observations of selected passages

We turn now to an exegetical study of several passages in 1 Corinthians where we can particularly discern elements of Paul's theology and thinking interacting either explicitly or implicitly with the pluralism which confronted him and the Corinthian Christians. The aim here is not to give a detailed exegesis of each passage in its entirety, but rather to make observations concerning those elements that most serve to illuminate Paul's response to his pluralist context and its undergirding theological structure.

1 Corinthians 1:1–2

> 1 Paul, called to be an apostle of Christ Jesus by the will of God, and our brother Sosthenes, 2 To the church of God that is in Corinth, to those who are sanctified in Christ Jesus, called to be saints, together with all those who in every place call on the name of our Lord Jesus Christ, both their Lord and ours:

*(1) Paul's use of 'God' (*theos*)*

The first point to observe is one which is easily overlooked given that we live in a world where a number of the major world religions are monotheistic and our own Christian heritage makes the assumption of monotheism a commonplace, even among our non-Christian contemporaries. So it is easy to just pass by Paul's unadorned use of the word 'god' (*theos*) here, but this use of the unqualified singular is an unselfconscious expression of his monotheism. He does not need to further identify this God because for him there is only one God, the God of Israel.[7] Paul will elaborate on this later in the letter in chapter 8.

(2) Connection to Jesus Christ

Although Paul can use the word 'god' in an unqualified way because he is referring to the one and only God, we can see here

---

[7] Various strands of Hellenistic thought could use the singular *theos*, not only with reference to a particular god (made clear from context), but also as a reference to the supreme God, or to God conceived as a summing up of all the gods or as the one of whom all the gods were an expression. This is nevertheless

too how for Paul it is almost impossible to talk about this one God and not to mention Jesus in the same breath. Paul's natural reflex is to bring the word into connection with Jesus Christ. So Paul is not just 'an apostle by the will of God', he is 'an apostle of *Christ*, by the will of God', and in v 2 the phrase 'the church of God' is in apposition with 'those who are sanctified *in Christ*'. Already we can begin to see here what will become even clearer in chapter 8, namely, that for Paul monotheism is not an abstract conception of the inner unity of God, nor even merely an abstract statement of the uniqueness of God. The one God and Jesus Christ are intimately connected. Paul's concept of the uniqueness of God includes Jesus Christ.

(3) Paul's mission—sent by Jesus, by the will of God

It seems relatively clear from 1 Corinthians (and also for that matter 2 Corinthians) that Paul's apostleship has come under some question in Corinth. So it is not surprising that Paul begins his letter by asserting his apostleship and its divine origin —'Paul called to be an apostle of Jesus Christ by the will of God'. Paul's ministry as an apostle is based on God's call, which is the outworking of God's prior will. The phrase 'of Jesus Christ' is almost certainly a subjective genitive[8], emphasising the origin of Paul's apostleship.

There is a vast scholarly debate over the nature of the term 'apostle'. To what extent is it an office? To what extent is it a function? To what extent has it become a technical term? Paul's own understanding is given in 1:17: 'For Christ did not send me (*apésteilén me*; note the cognate) to baptise but to preach the gospel (*euangelizesthai*).' That is, a Christian apostle is one who is sent by Jesus Christ *himself* for the purpose of proclaiming the gospel. The nature of the gospel and its proclamation will be

---

[7] (*continued*) quite distinct from Paul's usage. Paul, for example, would not have countenanced the interchangeable use of the terms 'God' and 'gods' that this allowed and which is found in some Stoic and Epicurean writings. See B. W. Winter, 'In Public and Private. Early Christians and Religious Pluralism.' In *One God, One Lord. Christianity in a World of Religious Pluralism* (Eds A. D. Clarke and B. W. Winter; Grand Rapids: Baker, 1992) 125–48.

[8] See, e.g. G. D. Fee, *The First Epistle to the Corinthians* (Ed., F. F. Bruce, *NICNT*; Grand Rapids: Eerdmans, 1987) 30.

discussed later but for now it is significant to note that Paul's gospel called for an *exclusive* allegiance to Christ and the God of Israel. So Paul's claim that his mission as an apostle is by the will of God; that it is not only backed by God, but is his express plan and purpose, implies that the turning of people away from their ancestral religions to follow Christ exclusively is part and parcel of God's plan and will.

(4) The Corinthian gathering of God

Paul addresses the Corinthian Christians as 'the church (*ekklēsia*) of God'. The Greek word was an everyday word for a gathering or assembly.[9] It had been used in the LXX to refer to Israel as a gathered people (for example Deuteronomy 4:10 which recalls the gathering at Horeb). Its NT usage picks up this OT usage to speak of the community of believers in terms of their gatherings, as the newly constituted, eschatological people of God.

But whereas Israel gathered at Horeb, the focal point of the Christian gathering is Christ. So here Paul describes the church of God in Corinth, using an appositional phrase, as those who are sanctified or set apart in, or perhaps by, Christ Jesus. The church as the gathered people of God, therefore, is constituted in relation to Christ and is coterminous with those who are sanctified by Christ.

(5) The called saints–worldwide and inclusive

Paul adds a second appositional phrase to his address of the Corinthian believers as the church of God. They are not only sanctified by Christ Jesus, but are called to be saints, called in other words by God to be his holy people as was Israel in Exodus 19:5–6. However, probably to remind the Corinthians that their own calling by God to be his people is part of a much bigger picture, the following prepositional phrase shows that this privilege does not rest just with the Corinthians but also 'with all who in every place call upon the name of our Lord Jesus Christ, their Lord and ours'. The word *pas* (all, every) is used twice here, emphasising the universal nature of God's people. 'All who call

---

[9] See, e.g. Acts 19:32, 39, 41 where the word is used both of a riotous mob and a legal assembly.

on the name of our Lord' picks up OT passages such as Psalm 50:15; Gen 4:26; 12:8, and especially Joel 2:32 which speaks both of calling on the name of the Lord, and of the Lord's calling of his people:

> Then everyone who calls on the name of the LORD shall be saved; for in Mount Zion and in Jerusalem there shall be those who escape, as the LORD has said, and among the survivors shall be those whom the LORD calls. (Joel 2:32)

All of these OT references speak of calling on the name of Yahweh, and Paul's allusion to this idea with reference to Jesus once again shows how intimately connected God and Jesus are in Paul's thinking. Paul understands this 'all people' to be inclusive, that is 'all', not only Jews, may now call on the name of the Lord Jesus and find salvation in him.

Similarly it is possible to see in the reference to 'in every place' an allusion to Malachi 1:11. This suggestion is given greater weight in that this passage also seems to underlie 2 Corinthians 2:14–17 and Romans 15:14–21, where Paul thinks of his ministry to the Gentiles in priestly and sacrificial terms. Malachi 1:11 reads:

> For from the rising of the sun to its setting my name is great among the nations (i.e. Gentiles), and *in every place* incense is offered to my name, and a pure offering; for my name is great among the nations, says the LORD of hosts.

Paul sees these words of Malachi about a worldwide honouring of God's name coming to fulfilment through and in his apostolic mission of preaching the gospel of Christ, as Gentiles 'in every place' come to call on the name of the Lord Jesus Christ.

1 Corinthians 1:18–21

> 18 For the message about the cross is foolishness to those who are perishing, but to us who are being saved it is the power of God. 19 For it is written, 'I will destroy the wisdom of the wise, and the discernment of the discerning I will thwart.' 20 Where is the one who is wise? Where is the scribe? Where is the debater of this age? Has not God made

> foolish the wisdom of the world? [21] For since, in the wisdom of God, the world did not know God through wisdom, God decided, through the foolishness of our proclamation, to save those who believe.

(1) Literary context and outline

This passage falls within the first major section of the letter (1:10–4:21), in which Paul deals with the divisions and factions in the Corinthian church based on the report he has received from Chloe's people (1:11). He begins in v 10 with an appeal that the Corinthians cease their dissension. In vv 11–16 he recounts the specific nature of the problem about which he has been informed. The Corinthians appear to have divided themselves into competing factions, apparently on the basis of who had baptised them, for Paul makes a point of minimising this aspect of his ministry among them in vv 14–16. He insists rather that he was called to preach the gospel in v 17, and not with 'wisdom of word' (*en sophia logou*) lest the cross of Christ be emptied of its power. This is an indication that the Corinthians' estimation of the relative eloquence or wisdom of speech of various leaders may also have been a factor in their divisions. This verse is a transition into the passage on which we are focussing here (1:17–2:16). In this passage Paul contrasts human wisdom with the foolish preaching of the cross of Christ, which is the wisdom and power of God. Paul draws the conclusion that all human boasting and pride is excluded. In chapter 3 Paul then returns explicitly to his theme of divisions amongst the Corinthians. So this passage is part of Paul's attempt to deal with the problems of division, arrogance and spiritual elitism that seem to beset the Corinthian church.

(2) The wisdom of foolishness

In 1:18 Paul lays down his thesis which he will defend and expound in 1:19–2:5. It is a statement about 'the word of the cross' (*ho logos . . . ho tou staurou*). This is a reference to the gospel proclamation, highlighting its crucial content. This 'word of the cross' elicits a twofold evaluation. It is foolishness to those perishing, while the power of God to those being saved. The gospel creates an eschatological division among its hearers.[10]

The perceived foolishness of 'the word of the cross' relates both to its content and activity. In terms of content, it is a foolish message, focusing on the crucifixion of the Jewish Messiah in Palestine. The cross was an instrument of execution reserved for slaves and criminals and it was offensive, almost an obscenity in polite circles, the symbol of disgrace and utter humiliation. To suggest that God would save the world through a crucified man appeared ludicrous, and no amount of argument, no human wisdom could make the cross appear otherwise. The cross can for us become something of an abstraction, the 'battery' placed in our atonement theology to make it work, but we need to remember that Paul here nails the gospel firmly to a Roman instrument of execution and to the nitty gritty historical particularity of all that it entailed.

The foolishness of the 'word of the cross' is not just a matter of its content but also its mode of delivery—the activity of preaching. Paul says in verse 21 that God decided to save those who believe through 'the foolishness of the proclamation'. The word *kērygma*, as with the verbal form *kēryssein* which appears in v 23, denotes preaching activity and not simply content. 'Proclamation' in the ancient world was the work of the 'herald' (*kēryx*), whose task it was to make a public declaration of an event (whether laws, terms of peace, or royal announcements) on the authority of the king or god. The issue of authority was crucial. The authority of the herald's words depend totally on the authority of the one who has commissioned him. And this is exactly why the activity of preaching, no less than its content, is offensive and foolish.[11] Since, as Paul says in verse 21, the world refuses to acknowledge God, it does not recognise his authority, and thus for any herald to offer a public declaration in his behalf constitutes a foolishness. Also, as Beaudean notes,

> proclamation does not seek to convince the world on the basis of the world's own criteria. God . . . does not meet the

[10] J. W. Beaudean, *Paul's Theology of Preaching* (Ed. J. W. McClendon; Vol. 6, NABPR Dissertation Series. Macon: Mercer University Press, 1988), 96.
[11] Beaudean, 104.

> world on its terms, but he overturns its wisdom. And on the basis of the world's failure, God simply 'declares' his salvation as located in the cross of Christ.[12]

That is why Paul in 2:1–5 says he did not come with lofty words or wisdom (2:1) and that his word and proclamation were not with persuasive wisdom (2:4), but rather that he decided to know nothing among them except Jesus Christ and him crucified (2:2). Paul does not regard the essence of his preaching ministry as engaging the interest and attention of people by means of fine speech and wise words or discourse, rather it is a matter of proclaiming the message of Christ crucified and risen.

The 'word of the cross' then, both in its content and activity, is foolishness to those who are perishing. Yet Paul is also clear that it is the very power of God to those who are being saved. For God in his wisdom has decided to enact salvation through the foolish proclamation of the word of the cross. He saves those who believe the message, giving their allegiance to, and trusting in, Christ. This salvation therefore is at once universal in scope but exclusive in application. It is open to all who hear the message, but experienced only by those who believe.

(3) The foolishness of wisdom

God's choice of the foolish proclamation of the crucified Christ as his means of salvation is presented by Paul as an overthrowing of human wisdom. In 1:19 he quotes from Isaiah 29:14 to demonstrate that wisdom's overthrow was foreordained by God. The rhetorical questions of 1:20 make a similar point. God has reduced all human attempts at wisdom to folly, for as Paul says in 1:21, despite all its vaunted wisdom, the world stands impotently unable to know God through that wisdom. Human wisdom is unable to reach up to God. God will only be truly knowable to humankind through his self-revelation. So Paul in 2:1 describes the gospel as the mystery of God, an idea on which he elaborates in 2:6–16 where he speaks of the hidden wisdom of God now revealed through the Spirit to those who are spiritual. Paul has already identified this wisdom of God as the crucified Christ back in 1:24. God is known through believing the procla-

---

[12] Beaudean, 104.

mation of the gospel, not through any exercise of human wisdom, whether through philosophy or religion.

1 Corinthians 5:9–10; 6:9–11

> [9] I wrote to you in my letter not to associate with sexually immoral persons—[10] not at all meaning the immoral of this world, or the greedy and robbers, or idolaters, since you would then need to go out of the world.
>
> [9] Do you not know that wrongdoers will not inherit the kingdom of God? Do not be deceived! Fornicators, idolaters, adulterers, male prostitutes, sodomites, [10] thieves, the greedy, drunkards, revilers, robbers—none of these will inherit the kingdom of God. [11] And this is what some of you used to be. But you were washed, you were sanctified, you were justified in the name of the Lord Jesus Christ and in the Spirit of our God.

(1) Literary context

In 1 Corinthians 5 Paul takes up the issue of reported sexual immorality in the church. In 5:9–13 he seeks to clarify an instruction he had given the Corinthians in a previous letter. There he had told them not to associate with sexually immoral people. Here he clarifies this imperative as having reference to those who are immoral and bear the name 'brother', who claim to be Christian. Paul's intention was not that the Corinthians seek to withdraw from all immoral people. This, he implies, is an impossibility since the Corinthians would need to leave the world to avoid all immoral people.

In 6:1–8 Paul takes up the issue of lawsuits among the Corinthian believers and argues strongly for the inappropriateness of this behaviour. It is not fitting that believers should take each other to court before pagan judges. Paul then proceeds with a general warning against wrongdoing in 6:9–11.

(2) Christians in the world

The significance for our purposes of these passages is that they highlight Paul's understanding of the religiously and ethically pluralist setting in which the Corinthians found themselves. They will have daily contact with idolaters, those who worship other gods, and with those of different standards of morality, including different sexual morality. Paul does not expect the Corinthians to withdraw from associating with such people, though he does expect the Corinthian Christians to avoid engaging in immorality and idolatry. He clearly does not envisage that the Christians should form some sort of social ghetto in Corinth. It is likely, given Paul's concern for evangelism expressed in chapter 9 and his reference in 6:9–11 to the previous lives of some of the Corinthians, that he had associated, for the sake of the gospel, with those who may have been 'fornicators, idolaters, adulterers, male prostitutes, sodomites, thieves, the greedy, drunkards, revilers and robbers' (1 Cor 6:9b–10a).

(3) The exclusiveness of the kingdom of God

A further point to note is that idolaters are included in the list of those who will not inherit the kingdom of God in 6:9. Given the virtually universal use of idols in the worship of other gods in Paul's day, this amounts to saying that the worshippers of other gods will not find a place in the kingdom of God. The implication of 5:9–13, is that idolaters, along with others, will face the judgement of God. This exclusiveness is tempered by those magnificent words of Paul's in 6:11 testifying to the gracious mercy of God. The kingdom is open to even such as these, but only in association with Christ and by the Spirit of God.

1 Corinthians 8:1–11:1

(1) Literary context and outline

8:1–11:1 is a distinct unit in 1 Corinthians where Paul deals with an issue that the Corinthians themselves have raised with him in their letter. It is an issue that seems to have been dividing the congregation and which arises directly from their location in their religiously pluralistic city: Is it permissible for Christians to eat meat that has been previously offered to an idol? The related though distinct question was: Is it permissible for a Christian to attend a feast in an idol's temple? These were not merely academic questions facing the Corinthians as it is likely that most meat sold in the city had been previously offered in sacrifice before an idol, and much of the life of the city would have revolved around the temples and the feasts held in them.

Gordon Fee argues that the main issue on view in this section is the latter question of attendance at temple feasts.[13] However, a preferable reading is to see that in chapter 8 Paul deals initially with the former and more general question of eating food offered to idols. He turns to the second more specific question of attendance at temple feasts briefly in 8:10, before returning to it in more detail in chapter 10. In answering these two related questions Paul seeks to deal with what he sees is a more fundamental problem that this issue has exposed, namely the Corinthians' propensity to put their freedom and rights ahead of their obligation to act in love towards each other.

Paul's answer to the first question is a heavily qualified 'yes' as well as an impassioned plea to care for the person of weak conscience. It is permissible to eat meat that has been offered to an idol, but for the sake of a Christian brother or sister the Corinthians must be willing to curtail their personal freedom in this area by avoiding any activity that might lead the brother or sister to stumble, and so endanger their salvation.

In chapter 9 Paul uses himself as an example of someone who has foregone the right of payment for his ministry in order to put no stumbling block in the path of anyone's salvation. He firstly establishes his right to receive payment and support for his ministry in 9:1–14, but then in 9:15–18 indicates how he has renounced this right. Paul has no choice about proclaiming the gospel. He is under direct command of the Lord Jesus, but he does have a choice as to whether he accepts payment and here Paul exercises his freedom and does not accept money.

Paul goes on to describe his willingness to put his freedom at the service of others by seeking in the words of his famous phrase to become 'all things to all people, that by all possible means (he) might save some' (9:22b).

[13] Fee, 357–363.

In chapter 10 Paul answers the second question about attendance at temple feasts with a firm 'no way!'. Paul gives a strong warning based on the wilderness experience of Israel. The Corinthians' much vaunted freedom is not a freedom to flirt with idolatry, for to participate in a temple feast is to participate in the worship of the idol. In 10:23 Paul starts to draw his conclusions and in the process deals with a further issue of eating with unbelievers in their homes. Again Paul says you are free to eat with unbelievers and even to eat meat offered to an idol, but your freedom must be constrained by the welfare of others. 10:31–11:1 concludes the whole unit. The Corinthians are to do everything for the glory of God, putting others' salvation ahead of their personal freedom. They are to follow Paul's example, who is following the example of Christ.

We will look at three passages from this unit in more detail.

1 Corinthians 8:1–6

> 1 Now concerning food sacrificed to idols: we know that 'all of us possess knowledge.' Knowledge puffs up, but love builds up. 2 Anyone who claims to know something does not yet have the necessary knowledge; 3 but anyone who loves God is known by him. 4 Hence, as to the eating of food offered to idols, we know that 'no idol in the world really exists,' and that 'there is no God but one.' 5 Indeed, even though there may be so-called gods in heaven or on earth—as in fact there are many gods and many lords— 6 yet for us there is one God, the Father, from whom are all things and for whom we exist, and one Lord, Jesus Christ, through whom are all things and through whom we exist.

(1) Knowledge versus love

Paul introduces the topic of food offered to idols in 8:1 but immediately turns aside to discuss the issue of the true estimation of the relative value of knowledge versus love. This will form a foundation for Paul's argument throughout these chapters that personal freedom and the knowledge it entails must be constrained and controlled by love for others, and indeed love of God. More important than the Corinthians' proud knowledge is that they love God, and that God knows them.

(2) *Many gods and many lords?*

In 8:4 Paul returns to the specific issue of food offered to idols. He seems to be quoting the claimed knowledge of some in Corinth that 'an idol is nothing in the world' and 'there is no God but one'. These are the flip sides of the same monotheistic coin and Paul is in basic agreement as verse 7 implies, although he will qualify the first statement later in chapter 10. Some, such as Bruce Winter,[14] argue that 8:5–6 continues Paul's quoting of the Corinthians, but it seems much more likely that this is part of Paul's acknowledgment that what the Corinthians claim to 'know' is in fact true. 8:5–6 at first glance might suggest that Paul is allowing the existence of these many gods and indeed that he is putting forward a form of henotheism when he states that 'for us there is one God . . . and one Lord'. There may be many gods and lords, but Christians happen to worship this particular god and this particular lord. This is not very far removed from the relativism of 'Jesus is true for you Christians'. But two things count against this understanding. Firstly, with regards to the phrase 'so-called gods' (*legomenoi theoi*), comparison with the use of the participle form of *lēgo* in constructions similar to this one in other extant Greek literature indicate that this attribution of deity, was popular but erroneous.[15] These were no gods in reality, and the English 'so-called' captures the idiom well.

Secondly, Paul's description of God the Father and the Lord Jesus in 8:6 indicates the universal nature and extent of their work—these are no mere tribal deities. The Father is the one 'from whom *all* things come', the source of all creation, he is not just God for Christians. And Jesus Christ is the one 'through whom *all* things come', the agent of all creation. He is not just Lord for Christians.

(3) *One God, one Lord*

In relation to the phrase 'many gods and many lords' (*theoi polloi kai kyrioi polloi*), is there a distinction between the use of

[14] Winter, 'Theological and Ethical Responses', 220.
[15] Winter, 'Theological and Ethical Responses', 220.

these terms 'god' and 'lord'? What might be the implications for Paul's understanding of the place of Jesus? Winter[16] suggests on the basis of the extant evidence that the terms as used by Paul here are close synonyms. So, for example, *kyrioi* is the title given to quite a number of the gods whose statues were to be found in Corinth. In this case the ascription of the title Lord to Jesus is likely an ascription of deity. That *kyrios* was the standard LXX translation for the name of God further supports Winter's point.

Is there no distinction at all between the terms? And if not, hasn't Paul left monotheism behind for 'bitheism'? A suggestion of Tom Wright's is helpful here.[17] He notes that verse 6 seems to be an allusion to Deuteronomy 6:4–5, the Shema.

> [4] Hear, O Israel: The LORD our God, the LORD is one. [5] And you shall love the LORD your God with all your heart, and with all your soul, and with all your might.

In its LXX form, this basic statement of OT monotheism brings the two words *theos* and *kyrios* together with reference to the God of Israel. In glossing *theos* with 'the Father' and *kyrios* with 'Jesus Christ', Paul is implying that this most basic confession of OT monotheism must now be understood to include Jesus. God's oneness is being presented, not as a simple mathematical unity, but as a relational unity. That the Shema goes on to urge undivided love of God on the basis of his oneness, and that the love of God has already been mentioned in this context in 8:33 strengthens Wright's case for a conscious allusion to the Shema. Paul's use of these terms distinguishes the Father and Jesus, while at the same indicating that they share the same deity.

1 Corinthians 9:19–23

> [19] For though I am free with respect to all, I have made myself a slave to all, so that I might win more of them. [20] To the Jews I became as a Jew, in order to win Jews. To those

[16] Winter, 'Theological and Ethical Responses', 214.

[17] Wright, N. T. *The Climax of the Covenant: Christ and the Law in Pauline Theology* (1st ed. Edinburgh: T&T Clark, 1991) 125–32.

> under the law I became as one under the law (though I myself am not under the law) so that I might win those under the law. [21] To those outside the law I became as one outside the law (though I am not free from God's law but am under Christ's law) so that I might win those outside the law. [22] To the weak I became weak, so that I might win the weak. I have become all things to all people, that I might by all means save some. [23] I do it all for the sake of the gospel, so that I may share in its blessings.

(1) All things to all people . . .

In 9:1–18 Paul, using himself as an example for the Corinthians, has described how he has freedom, but it is a freedom to serve the unbeliever by preaching the gospel without obstacles and free of charge. In 9:19–23 he elaborates on the principle he has been enunciating. Paul is free, he belongs to no one, but he will make himself a slave to everyone in order to win as many as possible. And so Paul seeks to be 'all things to all people'. In other words, he has a willingness to accommodate himself to whatever social or cultural setting in which he finds himself.

Paul's motivation in this is not that he fit in, or even that he not offend (he is not just a conflict avoider), but rather that the gospel be allowed to receive a proper hearing. So if there is something about his behaviour that might prevent that, Paul will modify his behaviour to remove any obstacle in the way of his hearers. He is, if you like, a cultural chameleon. And his goal in all this is that 'by all possible means' he 'might save some' (9:22b).

Now there are of course limits to this principle. Paul is not suggesting that he would become immoral to win the immoral, as he makes clear in 9:20–21. Although he is not under the law of Moses, he is nevertheless not free from God's law but is under Christ's law. He is not free to compromise his allegiance to his Lord, but in matters of indifference he has complete freedom, a freedom that is not directed at preserving his own comfort zone or his own cultural sensibilities, but rather a freedom to put himself out for others' salvation. The Corinthians have been the beneficiaries of all this, not least through Paul's determination to bring them the gospel free of charge. In all this there is an implied imperative directed at the Corinthians to follow Paul's example in their relations with one another and with unbelievers.

(2) . . . that I might save some

What becomes clear from the logic of this passage is that Paul goes to such great lengths to gain the gospel the best possible hearing because he sees in that gospel the only hope of salvation for unbelieving men and women. Paul does not proclaim Christ as merely a better option among many paths leading to salvation. He is not advocating swapping brands of religion as an advertiser might advocate swapping washing powders. Rather, underlying and implied by this passage is a conviction that salvation is found only in Christ and it is this, along with his devotion to Christ, which drives Paul's concern for unbelievers to hear the gospel. Paul is consumed by passion[18] for the lost. So he will go to great lengths to put himself out for the salvation of others. In doing this he is doing nothing other than following the example of his Lord, who not only ate and drank with sinners and outcasts, but also died for their salvation. Undergirding and informing Paul's example, providing the pattern, is the example of Christ to which Paul directs the Corinthians' attention in 11:1 and also in 8:11.

1 Corinthians 10:14–22

> 14 Therefore, my dear friends, flee from the worship of
> idols. 15 I speak as to sensible people; judge for yourselves
> what I say. 16 The cup of blessing that we bless, is it not a
> sharing in the blood of Christ? The bread that we break, is
> it not a sharing in the body of Christ? 17 Because there is
> one bread, we who are many are one body, for we all par-
> take of the one bread. 18 Consider the people of Israel; are
> not those who eat the sacrifices partners in the altar?
> 19 What do I imply then? That food sacrificed to idols is
> anything, or that an idol is anything? 20 No, I imply that

[18] If I may borrow from the title of the work by P. T. O'Brien, *Consumed by Passion: Paul and the Dynamic of the Gospel* (Homebush West: ANZEA, 1993).

> what pagans sacrifice, they sacrifice to demons and not to God. I do not want you to be partners with demons. [21] You cannot drink the cup of the Lord and the cup of demons. You cannot partake of the table of the Lord and the table of demons. [22] Or are we provoking the Lord to jealousy? Are we stronger than he?

(1) Flee idolatry

The first half of chapter 10, including the passage we are focussing on here, is a sustained warning to the Corinthians arising from the experience of Israel in the wilderness when they were judged for their unfaithfulness and idolatry. The Corinthians are free, but not free to indulge themselves, and certainly not free to compromise their wholehearted devotion to God by flirting with idolatry. They are rather to flee idolatry, and so they are not to take part in the temple feasts: for sacred meals are a way of participating or fellowshipping with the god involved and in his or her worship. Paul uses two positive examples to make this point. The Lord's supper is a participation in Christ, a way of declaring our union with him. Likewise, in the temple worship of Israel, the worshipper shared in eating the sacrifice to show his involvement and commitment to Yahweh. So it is, Paul argues, with pagan temple feasts. To share in these meals is to participate in the worship of the god in whose honour they are held, and this is to compromise a wholehearted allegiance to the Lord. The Corinthians are to flee such idolatry.

(2) Not God but demons

In verse 19, Paul in his typical way (*ti oun*) imagines an objector disparaging what he has said: 'Paul you're worried over nothing–what after all is a little food offered to an idol? Or the idol itself—haven't you already said that an idol is nothing in all the world? What you're saying implies that the gods represented by the idols exist after all.' To this objection Paul gives a reply that sounds quite immoderate to our modern sensibilities. Literally, 'What they offer in sacrifice is to demons and not to God.' It is true that the idols are not gods in any ultimate sense, but there is a spiritual reality underlying pagan worship, nevertheless. Their offerings are made to demons.

Now Paul's point can be obscured somewhat for us because of the connotations the word 'demon'. In the Greek speaking world of Paul's day the word demon (*daimonion*) denoted a lesser spiritual being, inferior to the major deities. It did not necessarily have the negative connotations that we ascribe to it. So, for example, in Acts 17, when Paul begins preaching in Athens about Jesus and the resurrection, Luke records in v.18 some of Paul's hearers as saying, 'He seems to be a proclaimer of foreign demons'. So Paul is taken to the Areopagus to explain his teaching. For Christians, and indeed Jews, spiritual beings which usurp the worship that is due to God alone are evil. But Paul is also positing the reality, yet inferiority, of the spiritual beings that underlie the pagan worship of Corinth. So for the Corinthians to engage in these temple feasts is to associate themselves in the worship of real, though inferior, spiritual beings, and so to compromise their single hearted devotion to God.

Paul is clear that pagan worship, in being offered to these demonic beings, is not being offered to the one true God. Paul does not accept the notion that ultimately behind all human religious activity is the one true God. He does not accept the Stoic idea that the various gods and spiritual beings are ultimately expressions or manifestations of the one God. The worship of unbelievers, directed to their gods, is not somehow worship of the one true and living God in disguise. In this regard Paul does not see non-Christian religion as a neutral thing. To worship other gods is *not* to worship the one true God and is therefore to fail to give him the honour that is his due. It is an affront to him.

(3) The jealousy of the Lord

Paul concludes his argument regarding attendance at the temple feasts with the rhetorical questions in 1 Cor. 10:22

> Or are we provoking the Lord to jealousy? Are we stronger than he?

Christians who attend the temple feasts are participating in idolatrous activity and sharing in the worship of demons. In doing this Paul suggests that they are provoking the Lord to jealousy. God is frequently in the OT described as jealous for his honour and his people's single-hearted devotion, but Paul's words here and in verse 20 specifically recall Deuteronomy 32:17–22, part of the song of Moses which he teaches Israel before he dies and which predicts Israel's unfaithfulness and the judgement of exile that will come upon her.

> 17 They sacrificed to demons, not God, to deities they had never known, to new ones recently arrived, whom your ancestors had not feared. 18 You were unmindful of the Rock that bore you; you forgot the God who gave you birth. 19 The LORD saw it, and was jealous he spurned his sons and daughters. 20 He said: I will hide my face from them, I will see what their end will be; for they are a perverse generation, children in whom there is no faithfulness. 21 They made me jealous with what is no god, provoked me with their idols. So I will make them jealous with what is no people, provoke them with a foolish nation. 22 For a fire is kindled by my anger, and burns to the depths of Sheol; it devours the earth and its increase, and sets on fire the foundations of the mountains.

The reference to strength in Paul's second rhetorical question also flows out of Deuteronomy 32. The question of Israel's participation in idolatry and the Lord's jealousy and discipline is set in terms of strength and power. God's judgement will impress on Israel both his strength and her lack of strength. God will only act to vindicate his people when their strength is completely gone.[19]

Verse 22 of chapter 10 brings the discussion of 10:1–22 to a head by sounding a solemn note of warning to the Corinthians not to defy God and tempt him to judgement. Amidst the pressures to be open, tolerant and accommodating to other faiths, some at least of the Corinthians have been unaware of the real danger to which their flirting with idolatry exposed them. God is not neutral with regard to the worship of other gods, nor even mildly disapproving. It arouses his jealousy and risks his judgement.

---

[19] B. Rosner, ' "No Other Gods". The Jealousy of God and Religious Pluralism', *One God, One Lord. Christianity in a World of Religious Pluralism* (A. D. Clarke and B. W. Winter, eds; Grand Rapids: Baker, 1992) 155.

Pluralism, preaching and Paul

Having surveyed the above passages from 1 Corinthians, we can now discern something of the shape of Paul's theological response to the pluralism of Corinth and some of the implications there might be for us in our pluralist setting.

(1) The one true God

Paul is absolutely clear that there is only one true and living God, the creator and source of all things, and that that God is the God of Israel who demands the undivided allegiance of his people. They are not to worship other gods.

Other gods are not alternative gods, nor are they alternative expressions or manifestations of the one God. They are in fact not real gods at all in any ultimate sense, but in so far as there is a spiritual reality underlying them, they are merely inferior spiritual beings, 'demons' who are not to be worshipped.

This has implications for Christians in a relativist setting where the pressure will be on for us to participate in watered down, lowest common denominator religion, and to worship a watered down, lowest common denominator God. This is especially true on public occasions where there is a desire for an expression of 'civic religion', for example in citizenship ceremonies. Different religions do not pray to the same God in different guises, and to accede to this view by dropping Christian distinctives in public prayer, for example, is not to offer Christian prayer. Better to refuse an opportunity to lead in public prayer if it is conditional on compromising that way.

Because, as Paul says in 1 Corinthians 10:26, quoting Psalm 24, 'the earth and its fullness are the Lord's', other so-called gods need not be feared, and can't contaminate food which may have been offered before an idol. Likewise, because there is only one true God we can have confidence in his sovereignty to achieve his purposes in the world. God and his purposes cannot be thwarted by rival spiritual powers.

In summary, Paul has a robust monotheism, that does not deny that spiritual realities may underlie other religions, but which nevertheless eschews syncretism and relativism.

(2) The uniqueness of Christ

For Paul, Jesus Christ is not one among many religious leaders, not even one from among the prophets of Israel, nor is he a second god. Rather he is the Lord, through whom all things came, and who shares in the very deity of God the Father.

At the same time he is the one who died nailed to a Roman cross in Palestine around AD 30. The historic particularity of Jesus' life, death and resurrection are essential parts of the gospel. He cannot be abstracted out of this setting. Sometimes in response to the pressures of relativism some have tried to do just that, to extract Christ out of his historical and cultural setting, to find the cosmic Christ, the Christ principle in all religions, and so on. But there is no 'cosmic Christ' or 'Christ principle' that can be distinguished from the man who died on the cross.

Related to this is the idea that the gospel is not primarily a set of theological abstractions, but a story, a heralding of events. Any proclamation of the gospel that fails to do justice to the historical and cultural particularity of Christ and his cross must be flawed.

(3) The foolishness of the gospel

The gospel is not open to ratification by human wisdom. From a human perspective the gospel will always appear foolish. We should expect this and not be embarrassed by it, nor let it undermine our confidence in the gospel and its proclamation. Newbigin expresses it well when he says that the gospel doesn't conform to the reigning plausibility structures of our age.[20] Paul would lead us to expect that it never will, for in the wisdom of God the world will not know God through its own wisdom and this is always the case.

Therefore any increased discomfort we feel as Christians in preaching the gospel due to the developments of post-modernism probably has more to do with the battle lines shifting when we had grown used to our modernist trenches, than to any real escalation in the battle. It is not that the gospel was credible and has now been made to seem foolish by the relativism of pluralism. It has always seemed foolish by whatever criteria the world presumes to judge it.

[20] Newbigin, 8–11.

Post–modernism dethrones autonomous human reason and has given up in despair at the possibility of human reason discerning ultimate truth. This is one aspect of post-modernism where we can say, 'Hear! Hear!' The impotence of human wisdom to know God is something we wish to affirm along with Paul, and it is a positive thing that many in our society have had their eyes opened to the limits of human wisdom.

There is a poem often told in support of the denial of normative truth, about six learned blindmen who each try to understand an elephant but fail dismally.[21] One feels the trunk and thinks the elephant is like a snake, one feels a leg and thinks the elephant is like a tree, and so on. These learned men are blind to the fact that they haven't discovered the whole truth, the point being that religions are much the same. They each think they've grasped the truth to the exclusion of others, but they need to acknowledge that they only each have part of the truth, not the whole truth. The flaw in this is that the poem only 'works' because there is someone outside the situation who can see the whole, who can see the groping attempts at knowledge of the learned blind men, and from that perspective can narrate the poem. The narrator does have the complete picture and can give a word from the outside. Paul says that God has delivered a word from the outside. Human wisdom may blindly grope after the truth, but the Christian gospel makes no claim to being the assured results of human wisdom and insight, but rather a word from God, a word once hidden and secret but now revealed, a word from the outside.

The fact that we have this knowledge of God, not through our own wisdom but through the gospel, means that it is possible to make absolute truth claims without personal arrogance. Indeed Christians have no grounds at all for arrogance in their dealings with unbelievers. Because of their pride Paul reminds the Corinthians of their human unimpressiveness (1 Cor 1:26–31). It is as well that we too recall that part of the gospel's foolishness is the kind of people God chooses to save through it.

---

[21] Carson, 123.

(4) The power of the gospel

All human attempts to know God will inevitably fail for God has decided to save those who believe through the foolishness of the proclamation of Christ crucified. Therefore, that is where we need to place our confidence in our evangelism, for the gospel, the word of the cross, is the power of God to save people (cf Rom 1:16–17). Because the gospel message and its preaching is foolish we will be constantly tempted to put our trust elsewhere. But we need to remember that the power to save does not lie in debate, or argument, or philosophical or apologetic discourse, or in a well polished church service, or even in a Christian education—good though these things might be—but in the proclamation of Christ in the gospel. We must maintain our confidence in the power of the gospel!

(5) The universality of the gospel

God has decided to save all who believe through the foolishness of preaching Christ; salvation is open to all. We need to remember that in Corinth 'all' included 'fornicators, idolaters, adulterers, male prostitutes, sodomites, thieves, the greedy, drunkards, revilers and robbers.' We must be careful of denying this universality by consciously or unconsciously restricting our proclamation to those we judge more worthy or more likely to respond.

Geographically God's plan encompasses the world and his intention is that his name be honoured 'in every place', as men and women call on the name of the Lord for salvation. This plan involved the commissioning and sending of Paul as an apostle by Jesus. Although we are not apostles as Paul was, if we want God's name to be honoured, as we pray so often in the Lord's prayer, then we too must have a commitment to the world-wide mission of the gospel.

A further aspect of the universality of the gospel is its universal truth claims. Many today would argue, as does Stanley Samartha, that 'a particular religion can claim to be decisive for some people, and some people can claim that a particular religion is decisive for them, but no religion is justified in claiming that it is decisive for all.'[22] Christianity makes just such a claim, though this claim cannot be justified on the basis of any human wisdom. To this extent Samartha is right. But the universal truth claim of Christianity is established not by human wisdom, but by its author, who is also the author of the universe itself.

(6) The exclusivity of the gospel

As there is only one true God who brooks no rivals and who demands single hearted allegiance, syncretism and relativism are not Christian options. Christ makes exclusive claims on our loyalty. His relationship to God is such that to reject him and the message of his cross cannot be other than to reject God.

Dialogue with other religions for the purpose of mutual understanding is desirable, but any dialogue which requires a prior denial of the exclusivity of Christ's claims must be unacceptable, as will any activity that involves participation in worship of other gods. We are to flee idolatry. Therefore, participation in inter-faith services and similar events which involve worship or acknowledgment of other gods, or even of a syncretistic lowest common denominator god, is not a faithful option for the Christian who is called to an exclusive allegiance to Christ.

Secondly, Christ is the one through whom the people of God are now constituted. It is through the message of Christ and him crucified that people find salvation and are set apart for God. There is no clear indication in Paul's thought of any hope outside of Christ, indeed those who reject the word of the cross as foolishness are explicitly said to be perishing. Whatever truth other religions may have, it is completely inadequate to enable people to know and so find salvation. In God's wisdom the world cannot know him through its own wisdom.

(7) The imperative of the gospel

As salvation is tied up with Christ and the proclamation of the gospel, the activity of proclamation is an imperative. Paul had

---

[22] S. Samartha, *Courage for Dialogue: Ecumenical Issues in Inter-Religious Relationships* (Geneva: World Council of Churches, 1982) 153.

an explicit commission of Jesus to preach the gospel ('woe to me if I do not preach', 1 Cor 9:16) that we do not have, but it is not necessary to have his direct commission to feel the same passion for the lost. This is not to say that every Christian must be a preacher, but every Christian should be concerned for evangelism and mission, if they are to be like Paul, and if they are to be like Christ.

Paul's passion for the lost led him to become 'all things to all people' that they may be saved, to put himself out for the sake of others' salvation, and to put his freedom at the service of others by being willing to cross cultural boundaries. Paul's imperative to follow his example (1 Cor 11:1), and the example of Christ, must challenge us with the question of our willingness to cross cultural boundaries as individuals and churches. Are we willing to budge from our comfort zones for the sake of the gospel?

(8) The pluralism of the gospel

The gospel is inevitably enculturated by its very historic character, and the Christian faith will always find cultural expression, but Paul demonstrated in his own ministry that it was not culturally bound. That is to say, the gospel and the Christian faith that flows from it is culturally transferable. It can and does find a home in any and every human culture (even church cultures!). At the same time it is bound to no culture. Because it is not culturally bound, we can expect that churches will be to some degree culturally pluralist and diverse.

However, the Christian faith, as well as being culturally transferable, is also culturally critical. As well as finding a home in every culture, it will also critique every culture, as exemplified by Paul's critique of the idolatry and immorality that were present in Corinth and from which the Corinthians had been delivered by the gospel (1 Cor 6:9–11; 10:19–22). The Christian faith can do this, not out of blind arrogance, but because it is 'a word from outside', a word from the creator.

In addition, the gospel calls people to a higher allegiance than their culture. It does not ask them to leave their culture, but it will inevitably critique their culture, and it will alter their involvement in it. So the Corinthians were not called on by Paul to withdraw from the pagan and immoral society in which they were situated, but neither were they any longer free to participate in the idolatry and immorality around them. Also, because allegiance to Christ must come before allegiance to culture, Paul was free to become all things to all people by crossing cultural boundaries for the sake of the gospel. He was free to be a 'cultural chameleon'. This must raise for us the question of which cultural boundaries are we willing to cross, as individuals and as churches, if any at all? Are there cultural boundaries we are unwilling to cross? If there are we need to think hard about whether we have put culture, even our church culture, above Christ.

Finally, because allegiance to Christ must come before allegiance to culture, 'the all things to all people' principle must have limits. The boundaries that Paul sets for himself and the Corinthians are the law of Christ and fleeing idolatry (1 Cor 9:19–23). We are not free, in becoming all things to all people, to disobey Christ and his instruction, nor to be involved in anything that would mean participation in the worship of other gods.

Conclusion: Pluralism, preaching and us

> We affirm that there is only one Saviour and only one Gospel, although there are a wide variety of evangelistic approaches . . . We also reject as derogatory to Christ and the Gospel every kind of syncretism and dialogue which implies that Christ speaks equally through all religions and ideologies. Jesus Christ, being himself the only God-man, who gave himself as the only ransom for sinners, is the only mediator between God and man. There is no other name by which we must be saved . . .[23]

The exclusivism of this statement is offensive to many today for we live at the end of the 20th century in a pluralistic world, and a pluralistic nation. Though we may find the pluralism of our culture discomfiting and possibly threatening, it presents us with an opportunity and a challenge.

---

[23] J. Stott, 'The Lausanne Covenant' in *The Lausanne Covenant: An Exposition and Commentary* (Minneapolis: World Wide Publications, 1975) 14.

How, as Christians, should we respond to the pluralism we encounter? By surrender to the relativism all around us? That is what the world is calling us to do, to cease our evangelism, to drop all claims to exclusiveness, to beat our pulpits into dialogue tables. This would be to betray Christ.

Or shall we respond by withdrawing from our pluralist society into the comfort of the Christian ghetto? Will we retreat behind the barricades into our Christian communities, our Christian schools, our Christian sporting teams, and stare out at the world with fearful eyes, mounting an evangelistic foray every year or so to assuage our consciences with proof that we care for the lost, and so pay lip service to the universal rule of Christ, wondering why fewer and fewer people walk through our doors and our churches decline? I write as an Anglican. God is of course sovereign and the work of the gospel will go on, but I for one would find it a great sadness if our denomination were to become an evangelistic backwater while the stream of God's action passed us by because we held on to our fears or to our Anglican culture tighter than the gospel. In the end we cannot sit in a cultural ghetto without betraying Christ's mission.

How should we respond to the pluralism around us? Surrender? Withdrawal? Let me suggest a third option: engagement. Will we have the confidence in God's sovereignty, confidence in the gospel and its proclamation, to seek to engage with our society at every level without being conformed? Will we engage our contemporaries with the gospel of the crucified and risen Christ; to be all things to all people, so that by all possible means we might save some? May it be so.

Exploring further

1. What are the difficulties of preaching the Christian gospel in a modern pluralist setting? How can we be tempted to compromise the exclusive claims of Christ and surrender to the relativism of our society?
2. Is it possible for Christians to participate in ecumenical gatherings that involve worship of or prayer to a supposed common deity? What principles are involved?

3. How can we be tempted to accept the world's evaluation of the foolishness of preaching the gospel? Where else can we be tempted to place our confidence as we seek to win people to Christ? What is the antidote for this?
4. Do we reflect the universality of the gospel call in our evangelism? Are there people or groups we write off as 'beyond the pale'?
5. The paper suggests in its conclusion that engagement, rather than surrender or withdrawal, is the faithful response to the pluralism around us. Do you agree? Why or why not? What will such engagement involve?

3

Models of Mission and the Doctrine of the Spirit

Robert Doyle

Synopsis

Three models together cover the missiological thinking of the vast majority of Christian groupings. The episcopal model is based on the ideas of Ignatius of Antioch and Cyprian. It has as its foundation the view that the bishop is the sacrament of Christ, and therefore the necessity that the mission is the bishop's, in which others may participate as his vicars. The episcopal model is concerned to preserve a number of verities which the NT is also concerned for: a recognisable and orderly public ministry, a tradition (*paradosis*) from the apostles, a connectivity and mutual responsibility between Christian congregations, love, and unity in Christ's Church in the world. However, two criticisms may be levelled from the wider structures of Christian thought. The other two models spring from pneumatology. Charismatic and Pentecostal missiological thinking stresses that mission flows out of direct experience of the Holy Spirit who acts in empowering, gifting and directing. Gordon Fee argues that the presence of the 'charismata' is a necessary foundation for mission, and seems to make them a sacrament of the Spirit. A third model found in pneumatological writings from both Catholic and Protestant theologians, offers another perspective. The work of the Spirit is viewed on a universal horizon, finding expression in the spirituality of different cultures. This has profound implications for dialogue with other religions and cultures. The work of T. F. Torrance, on the pneumatology of the theologians of the ancient catholic church and of the Bible, suggests five basic statements about the doctrine of the Spirit, and four corollaries for knowledge of God, and thus for understanding mission as the increase of knowledge of God in the world. The paper concludes with consequences for thinking about mission.

'Receive this charge which is yours and mine'

These are the words of institution to the cure of souls by the bishop to a priest taking up a benefice or a parish in the Church of England.[1] In this form they date from the late twelfth century, but in them stands an understanding of mission whose roots are in the early second century of the Christian era, just decades from the time of the apostles. It is a view of mission which is not only dominant in the present day Anglican communion, but is also the outlook of the great majority of the denominations of the Christian world. It is a doctrine of mission, which in summary form, states that Christian mission is rightly and exclusively the bishop's. Rightly operating, others are but participating in that episcopal mission as his representatives or vicars. The foundation of this view is the belief that the bishop is the sacrament of Christ.

There is another view of mission which arguably is also as old, and is certainly of enormous contemporary influence, that 'the Holy Spirit is the originator and impetus for world mission, and if Christians are to experience the Holy Spirit personally, then . . . the natural outflow of this personal experience is involvement in the world mission of the Holy Spirit.' Behind this view is the belief that 'Jesus Christ is personally present as the Lord of the world harvest in the experience of empowerment for this harvest.' Christ is 'the Baptizer in the

---

[1] H. W. Cripps, *A Practical Treatise on the Law Relating to the Church and Clergy*, 8th ed. (London: Sweet and Maxwell, 1937) 270–1. The full words of institution read: *Instituo te ad tale beneficium, habere curam animarum, et accipe curam tuam et meam.*

Holy Spirit'.[2] This is the accepted Charismatic and Pentecostal doctrine of mission,[3] and, implied in its resonance with certain statements in the NT, is an alternative to and critique of the first view.

Further, a pneumatological approach is also now characteristic of both Catholic and Protestant missiologies more widely considered. These employ the notions of *Spiritus Creator* and *theologia religionum* (the theology of religions) to set religion and pneumatology in a global and communitarian context. Therefore, we ought to expect the Holy Spirit to be operating in other religions. Furthermore, Christian mission of the overt kind can expect to meet the Holy Spirit in other religions as such mission engages with them.

In this paper I want to explore the intent and meaning of these two influential views, and then critique them against the doctrine of the Spirit which is apparent in the writings of the Fathers of the Councils of Nicaea and Constantinople and has its ground in the teaching of the NT.

'Without the bishop you should do nothing'

In the first decade of the second century, Ignatius, Bishop of Antioch, under guard of ten soldiers, was escorted from Antioch to his martyrdom in Rome. During this time he wrote seven letters in which he laid down an understanding of ministry that centred on the three-fold order of bishops, priests and deacons. These three orders are the *typoi* or mystical types and representation of the redemptive acts of the Father sending the Son, and the Spirit-filled apostles proceeding from both.[4] Using the notions of 'types' and 'representations' which are familiar to

---

[2] L. G. McClung, 'Missiology', in *Dictionary of Pentecostal and Charismatic Movements*, ed. S. M. Burgess and G. B. McGee (Grand Rapids: Zondervan, 1988) 607.

[3] More widely, see: M. J. Glaxiola, 'The Pentecostal Ministry', *International Review of Mission* 66 (1977) 57–63; W. J. Hollenweger, 'After Twenty Years Research on Pentecostalism', *International Review of Mission* 75 (1986) 3–12; J. N. Saracco, 'The Type of Ministry Adopted by the Pentecostal Churches in Latin America', *International Review of Mission* 66 (1977) 64–70.

[4] A. Brent, *Cultural Episcopacy and Ecumenism: representative ministry in church history from the age of Ignatius of Antioch to the Reformation with special reference to contemporary ecumenism* (Leiden: E. J. Brill, 1992) 88.

Hellenic thought, Ignatius makes the closest tie possible between the work of God in Christ (during Christ's earthly ministry and now in his heavenly location), the Christian community, and present Christian ministry, such that our very salvation depends on obedience to the bishop:

> . . . let all reverence the deacons as an appointment of Jesus Christ, and the bishop of Jesus Christ, and the presbyters as the sanhedrin of God, and assembly of the apostles. Apart from these, there is no Church.[5]

> Since therefore I have, in the persons before mentioned [bishop Damas, presbyters Bassus and Apollonius], beheld the whole multitude of you [the church of the Magnesians][6] in faith and love, I exhort you to study to do all things with a divine harmony, while your bishop presides in the place of God, and you presbyters in the place of the assembly of the apostles, along with your deacons, who are most dear to me, and are entrusted with the ministry of Jesus Christ, who was with the Father before the beginning of time, and in the end was revealed . . . Let nothing exist among you that may divide you; but be ye united with your bishop, and those that preside over you, as a type and evidence of your immortality.[7]

> Be ye subject to the bishop, and to one another, as Jesus Christ to the Father, according to the flesh, and the apostles to Christ, and to the Father, and to the Spirit; that so there may be union both fleshly and spiritual.[8]

> . . . ye are subject to the bishop as to Jesus Christ . . . so without the bishop you should do nothing . . .[9]

---

[5] Ignatius, 'To the Trallians', *ANCL* (Edinburgh: T & T Clark, 1867) volume I, p 67, section iii.

[6] This theme of beholding the church in the person of the bishop is recurrent in the letters. See, 'To the Ephesians' sections i, v; 'To the Magnesians' ii, vi; 'To the Trallians' i, iii.

[7] Ignatius, 'To the Magnesians', *ANCL*, I.61. vi.

[8] Ignatius, 'To the Magnesians', *ANCL*, I.64–5.xiii; cf Ignatius, 'To the Ephesians', *ANCL*, I.50–51.iv.

[9] Ignatius, 'To the Trallians', *ANCL*, I.66.ii.

This view of the work of God and the nature of the Christian community being centred in the bishop by ontological necessity was to be deepened, widened, and then narrowed. The deepening happened through the flowing together of the work of Irenaeus (130–200) on the notion of a fixed *paradosis*, the teaching of the apostles handed down from one generation to another in the person of the bishops, and of the understanding of Tertullian (160–225) that catholicity or correctness of doctrine not only rests on strict apostolic succession for the existence of a particular church but also 'a kinship in doctrine' (*pro consanguinitate doctrinae*) to the apostolic standard.[10] The narrowing occurs in the work of Tertullian's theological successor, Cyprian (d. 258), who wrote a treatise, *On the Unity of the Church*, the only monograph on the nature of the Church until the time of the Reformation. In a church divided by the Novatianist schism, Cyprian emphasises 'the unity of the church through the mutual intercommunion of the one valid bishop in every place, who alone can succeed his predecessor'. Further, the bishop locally incarnates the episcopal office or college with which he is joined, 'to which, and for the sake of which, obedience is required from clergy and laity alike'.[11] In this way, Cyprian shows a desire for a unity which in his late interpreters becomes a 'monolithic unity':

> This unity we ought firmly to hold and assert, especially those of us that are bishops who preside in the Church, that we may also prove the episcopate itself to be one and undivided . . . The episcopate is one, each part of which is held by each one for the whole. The Church also is one, which is spread abroad far and wide into a multitude by an increase of fruitfulness . . . As there are many rays of the sun, but one light . . . Thus also the Church, shone over with the light of the Lord, shed forth her rays over the whole world, yet it is one light which is everywhere diffused, nor is the unity of the body separated. . . . She broadly expands her rivers, liberally flowing, yet her head is one, her source one; and she is one mother, plentiful in the results of her

---

[10] Tertullian, *De. Praes. Haer*. 32; cited from Brent, 155.

[11] Brent, 158.

> fruitfulness: from her milk we are born, by her milk we are nourished, by her spirit we are animated . . . She appoints the sons whom she has born for the kingdom. Whoever is separated from the Church and is joined to an adulteress, is separated from the promises of the Church; nor can he who forsakes the Church of Christ attain to the rewards of Christ. He is a stranger; he is profane; he is an enemy. He can no longer have God for his Father, who has not the Church for his mother.[12]

Now, for catholicity and thus recognition of brotherly activity to occur, consanguinity in doctrine or even possession of a bishop is not enough. With later developments of Cyprian's position by Augustine (354–430), and apically by Gregory VII (d. 1085), the 'glue' which holds Christians together in the saving ark of the Church must be not just possession of and faithfulness to the *paradosis* of doctrine, nor even adherence to a local bishop, but recognition of and by a formal episcopal jurisdiction. After all, both the Novatianists of Cyprian's time and the Donatists of Augustine's were orthodox in doctrine, although rigorist in discipline, to a degree that denied the evangelical doctrine of repentance at an even deeper level than the legal repentance which prevailed in the wider Catholic church.[13] And they were, of course, endlessly irritating, as they croaked 'like frogs in the marshes, "we are the only Christians".'[14]

Before suggesting a critique, it needs to be noted that by this episcopal understanding of church and mission, Ignatius, Irenaeus, Tertullian and Cyprian sought to safeguard certain verities which are central to the NT, and which we, if we are to advance an alternative view of mission, will need to safeguard too. Throughout their relevant writings we see a concern that there should be a recognisable and orderly public ministry of the gospel, that there is indeed a tradition or *paradosis* from the

---

[12] Cyprian, 'On the Unity of the Church', *ANCL* (Grand Rapids: Eerdmans, c. 1851), vol. V, pp 422–23, section v–vi.

[13] For the development of the notion of repentance from Tertullian onward, see my 'Repentance', in *Explorations 9, Responding to the Gospel: Evangelical Perspectives on Christian Living*, ed. B. G. Webb, (Adelaide: Open Book, 1995) 15–39.

[14] Augustine, *Narr. in Psa.* 95,11; cited from Brent, 173–74.

apostles which God in Christ has put his very own stamp or character on, that this should be handed on faithfully without addition or subtraction, and that there is necessarily a connectivity and mutual responsibility between Christian congregations which is visible and apostolic, Also there must be love, and especially, unity in Christ's church in the world. One does not have to spend much time reflecting on say, Paul's letter to the Ephesians, and his pastoral epistles, to feel the urgency and impress of these concerns.

Two lines of criticism suggest themselves. Firstly, from the wider structures of Christian thought itself, the pagan ontologies of being that must be presumed, in the belief that the mission is the bishop's, crumble before that trinitarian ontology which comes from the gospel. That is, unlike the assumptions governing the Ignatian-Cyprian axis, real being is neither hierarchical as it is in pagan Greek thought, nor is it legal-political as it is in ancient Rome, but real being is a participation in being.[15] It is interesting that when Tertullian's rigorism and temperament had placed him outside the Catholic church, he too appeals to a specifically Christian and trinitarian ontology to assert that he is a member of the Church of Christ:

> The church itself is, properly and principally, the Spirit himself, in whom is the trinity of the one divinity, Father, Son and Holy Spirit. [The Spirit] gathers (*congregat*) that church which the Lord has made to consist in 'three'. And so . . . every number which has combined together into this faith is accounted by its author and sanctifier.[16]

Although, as Colin Gunton indicates, the point is obscure and the Latin is almost untranslatable, Tertullian is clearly drawing links between three terms: the Trinity, the community of faith, and its free act of congregating.[17]

Allied with this, the truth that God does not operate sacramentally in the world (which is not the same as saying that he

---

[15] See especially, C. E. Gunton, *The Promise of Trinitarian Theology*, (Edinburgh: T & T Clark, 1991) chs 3 and 4.

[16] *De Pudicitia*; cited from Gunton, 63.

[17] Gunton, 63.

may not operate through sacraments), but directly in person, undercuts the power of the foundational assertion that the bishop is a sacrament of Christ. That is, in the person and work of the Spirit, who preaches the gospel, God as Father, Son and Holy Spirit does his missionary work directly and personally, with or without bishops.[18]

In the light of Tertullian's comments the second line of criticism may sound superfluous. I want to make two simple observations from Luke–Acts. First, the need to validate a mission by a tight connectivity to the apostolic band seems not to be on view in Luke 9:49–50 when, after John takes umbrage at an outsider casting demons out in Jesus name, Jesus commands: 'Do not stop him; for whoever is not against you is for you.' Neither does Paul appear worried by the somewhat freelance ministry of Apollos, who not only appears unconnected to the apostles, but also has a defective baptism (Acts 18:24–19:1)! Secondly, in Acts especially, it is the Holy Spirit who appears to be the missioner, or at least, the chief missioner. So, in Acts 8:26–40, it is an angel of the Lord and the Spirit of the Lord who directs Philip. In Acts 5:17–32, after an angel of the Lord releases the apostles from prison, they then bear witness, with the Holy Spirit, to the death and resurrection of Jesus. At the turning point of Peter's understanding about the mission to the Gentiles, the Spirit speaks to him in a vision (Acts 10:19; 10:12). It is the Holy Spirit who is credited with baptising Cornelius and his household into the hope of Israel (Acts 11:15). The Spirit sets aside Barnabas and Saul and thrusts them out into missionary work (Acts 13:2,4). It is the Spirit who forbids Paul's apostolic band from speaking in Asia Minor, and calls them instead to Europe. It is the Spirit's decision about the Gentile mission which prevails at the Jerusalem Council (Acts 15:28; cf. 15:8; 13:2; 11:12).

Where do these observations lead us, and especially the second one, concerning the role of the Spirit? Perhaps unsurprisingly, both Ignatius and Cyprian, the two most

---

[18] Refer my, 'The Spirit of the Father and the Spirit of the Son', in *Explorations 6: Spirit of the Living God* (Part II), ed. B. Webb (Sydney: Lancer, 1992) 19–48; 'Word and Sacrament in catholic and evangelical theology', in *Who May Celebrate? Boundaries of Anglican Order*, ed. I. Head (Sydney: Standing Committee of General Synod of the Anglican Church of Australia, 1996) 8–19.

responsible for the foundations of the episcopal model of ministry, make little and only passing reference to the Holy Spirit, although they do talk quite fully about the person and work of Christ. May not a little further reflection on the person and work of the Spirit not only throw more light on the nature of mission, but also on the verities that the episcopal model is seeking to protect, that is, the importance of *paradosis*, handing it on, unity and the like?

The pneumatological model of mission

It is of course the modern Charismatic and Pentecostal movement which has thrust the importance of pneumatology onto centre stage. The pneumatological aspect of their missiology can be summed up in these terms:

> For Pentecostals, the Holy Spirit is personally active, living in and directing his servants in world evangelization (Acts 8; 13). Missiologically speaking, the Holy Spirit is not just a force or influence but is also personally and powerfully potent on the frontiers of mission.[19]

The direct activity of the Spirit in mission is seen in three ways which are distinctive to the movement: empowerment, gifting and direction. All of these fall within a definitive two phase understanding of the work of God, the cross and Calvary followed by the donation of the Spirit at Pentecost.[20] These themes have been explored well and often enough so as not to need further elaboration here, but it is of interest to note the emphasis that is apparent in Gordon Fee's treatment of 'gifting'.

Fee stresses that the fulfilment of the promised blessing for the Gentiles lies 'in their having experienced the Spirit as a living and dynamic reality'. He continues:

---

[19] McClung, 607.

[20] See J. R. Williams, *Renewal Theology: the Church, the Kingdom, and the Last Things*, vol. 3, (Grand Rapids: Zondervan, 1992) 145–151; McClung, 607–9; G. D. Fee, *Paul, the Spirit, and the People of God*, (Peabody, Mass.: Hendrickson, 1994); and for a more reflective and self-critical approach, Tom Smail's 'A Renewal Recalled' in Tom Smail, Andrew Walker, and Nigel Wright, *Charismatic Renewal: the search for a theology*, (London: SPCK, 1993) 7–21.

> The blessing of Abraham, therefore, is not simply 'justification by faith'. Rather, it refers to the life of the future now available to Jew and Gentile alike, achieved through the death of Christ but applied through the dynamic ministry of the Spirit—and all of this by faith.[21]

If we ask, what is this 'living and dynamic reality', Fee's answer lies in terms of individual conversion, and the coming into existence of Christian community, 'who will live the life of the future in their present existence together as they await the consummation'.[22] As well as the paradigmatic presence of the 'fruits of the Spirit', the presence and exercise of the *charismata* in the context of worship is normative for this life of the future experienced now.[23] Without the latter, the Church too often has been narrow, inward looking and institutionalised, while the state of the believer has been one of 'spiritual disease and feebleness'.[24]

Fee's emphasis on the gifts, and the sad results of their contemporary loss, is also a major thematic consideration in his commentary on 1 Corinthians. Indeed, on exegetical grounds he argues that the 'grace' of 1 Corinthians 1:4–2:18 is not the gracious outpouring of God's mercy in Christ toward the undeserving, but the *charismata,* which are the concrete expressions of God's gracious activity in his people.[25] When this sustained emphasis is placed alongside another peculiarity of Fee's commentary, an interesting result is discernible. Fee does not directly apply the exclusive aspect of Paul's cruciocentric resolve of 1 Corinthians 1:4–2:18, and especially of 2:2, to the problems of the Corinthian church. 'The foolishness of the preaching of the cross' is just treated historically. The 'foolishness' applies only to pagan Greeks and the over-politicised messianic expectations of Judaism. In the end, Fee reduces Paul's exclusive position on preaching the cross to, 'God doing things his way', and this in the main appears as his point of

---

21 Fee, *Paul,* 60.
22 Fee, *Paul,* 61, 66,67.
23 Fee, *Paul,* 152–92; esp 152–53, 173–77, 184–89.
24 Fee, *Paul,* 185–87.
25 Fee, *The First Epistle to the Corinthians,* (Grand Rapids: Eerdmans, 1987) 37.

departure for applying the teaching of Paul in 1 Corinthians to both the original and modern reader. Hence, it seems to me, Fee makes the presence and exercise of the spiritual gifts an indispensable sacrament of God's direct work in his church and thus in the world in mission.[26]

Other writings interested in pneumatology, especially but not exclusively by Roman Catholic theologians, also raise missiological questions. Contemporary views extend the 16th century understanding of Calvin that we ought credit the Spirit, 'as the sole fountain of truth', with giving us human sciences like jurisprudence, medicine, mathematics, and politics (*Ins* 2.2.15). Today, the work of the Spirit is seen not only in creation, but in religious experience in and beyond Yahwism, and even beyond the physical confines of Israel in the general history of religions from which Judaism springs as a special instance. Protestant writers like Hendrikus Berkhof and Catholic writers like Philip J. Rosato and Karl Rahner argue that such is the Spirit's role that Christian pneumatology can begin from the ethnology and sociology of religion as well as from the biblical witness. Thus approached it will be seen that 'in many cultures an inchoate notion of the immanent spirit of divine mystery produces greater social unity and clearer understanding of the cosmos and of life.'[27] Because the Holy Spirit is *Spiritus Creator*, pneumatology then should profitably spend time in dialogue with the social sciences, thus placing 'religion and pneumatology in a global and communitarian context from the outset'.[28] In this way, the work of the Spirit is viewed on a universal horizon as resulting in the history of religions and various expressions of spirituality in different cultures. Christians are urged to look with discernment beyond the usual sacramental and evangelical ministries of the church to see evidences of the Spirit's consummatory work elsewhere as he ushers in the new age, the new creation. This is seen as having profound implications not only for social involvement, but also for genuine dialogue with other religions and cultures.

---

26 Fee, *Corinthians*, 42–45, 74–78.

27 P. J. Rosato, 'Holy Spirit', in *A New Dictionary of Christian Theology*, ed. A. Richardson and J. Bowden (London: SCM, 1983) 263.

28 Rosato, 263.

Concomitant with this has been the development since the 1960s of the *theologia religionum*, the theology of religions. This has raised to a new level the question of the attitude Christians and Christian missions should adopt to other faiths and their adherents. *Nostra Aetate*, a document of Vatican II on the non-Christian religions, has generated much discussion in Roman Catholic missiology, in which such religions are described alternatively as 'ordinary ways of salvation', 'anonymous Christianity', or 'the latent Church'.[29] It is urged by D. T. Niles, Max Warren, and Kenneth Cragg, amongst others, that we go out in mission expecting to meet the God who has preceded us and has been preparing people within the context of their own cultures and convictions. As David Bosch summarises it: 'God has already removed the barriers; his Spirit is constantly at work in ways that pass human understanding.' We 'do not just "take him" to the others; he accompanies us and also comes toward us'.[30]

Perhaps a little surprisingly, this selective overview of modern pneumatological models of mission does not throw a great deal of light on the nature of mission in its episcopal form, nor on the verities that the episcopal model is seeking to protect, that is, the importance of *paradosis*, handing it on, unity and the like. Instead, as we seek to sketch a theology of mission acceptable to the NT witness we face another set of questions. The first two questions are about 'soils', if I may put it that way. Does Christian mission only appropriately proceed from a Christian congregation immersed in the experience of *charismata*, which may be properly seen as the second phase of determinative Christian experience? From the other side, may we expect the Spirit to be revealing God in other, non-Christian religions, awaiting our arrival with the gospel? Finally, since 'we do not have him in our pockets', to quote Bosch's description, ought a 'Gamaliel principle' operate as we observe

---

[29] D. J. Bosch, *Witness to the World: The Christian mission in theological perspective*, (London: Marshall, Morgan & Scott, 1980) 185; see also D. J. Bosch, *Transforming Mission: paradigm shifts in theology of mission*, (New York: Maryknoll, 1991) 474.

[30] Bosch, *Transforming Mission*, 484. See also Y. Congar, *I Believe in the Holy Spirit, volume II: 'He is Lord and Giver of Life'*, trans. D. Smith, vol. 2, (London: Geoffrey Chapman, 1983) 219.

freelance work proceeding, even outside the Christian religion itself?

Having identified some of the concerns and emphases of the episcopal and pneumatological models, I want still to pursue my hunch that pneumatology may in fact give us certain true pointers to a theology of mission. To do this, I will summarise the basic statements that T. F. Torrance has arrived at on the doctrine of the Spirit from a life time of reflection on the fathers of the ancient catholic church, and the Bible.

The doctrine of the Spirit on the basis of internal relations

It is one of Tom Torrance's distinctive contributions to patristics that he has discerned in the fathers of Nicaea-Constantinople, especially in Athanasius, that they arrived at their doctrine of the Spirit by rejecting the theological method characteristic of the Arians whereby knowledge of Christ and the Spirit was to be determined on the basis of God's external relations to the world.[31]

Arianism had demanded that the doctrine of God be exclusively understood on the basis of a movement back from his works to him as source, that is, on the basis of external relations. Athanasius insisted that we must understand God by approaching him through the Son and call him Father. Knowledge of God takes place through a movement of divine revelation from the Father through the Son in the Spirit, and, an answering movement of confession on our part, by faith, in the Spirit through the Son to the Father. The Arians attacked the true divinity of Jesus Christ because of the difficulties they saw posed by a neoplatonically conceived God relating to created matter. Athanasius answered them, not by solving for them the problem of God and creation by exploring external relations between God and his creation, but by clarifying the internal

[31] T. F. Torrance, *The Trinitarian Faith: The Evangelical Theology of the Ancient Catholic Church*, (Edinburgh: T & T Clark, 1993); 'Karl Barth and the Latin Heresy', *Karl Barth, Biblical and Evangelical Theologian* (Edinburgh: T & T Clark, 1990) 213–240.

relations within God himself as witnessed to by Holy Scripture, and asserting the *homoousion* between the Father and the Son as the foundation from which the problem had to be addressed, not a conclusion to be arrived at by deduction. Athanasius showed from Scripture that God had to be known through internal, not external relations; that is, God had to be known as Trinity.[32]

This method, the theology of internal relations, Athanasius also applied to the doctrine of the Spirit. That is, the Spirit was not to be conceived of on the basis of how he may appear in his mission in the world, broadly conceived, but on the basis of the fact that Holy Scripture tells us that we derive our knowledge of the Spirit from our knowledge of the Son. On this ground, the Spirit is the Spirit of the Father and the Son, and therefore *homoousion*, or consubstantial with them. When this is grasped, then we may turn our attention to how we should understand the Spirit's work in the world.

Let me then summarise the leading features of the doctrine of the Spirit which appear in Tom Torrance's scriptural appraisal of Athanasius, the Cappadocians, Cyril of Jerusalem, and perhaps above all, Epiphanius of Salamis (c.315–403) and Didymus the Blind (c.313–98).[33]

Five basic statements

(1) In the Spirit, God himself is immediately present in our midst; so that God himself is the content of what he does for us and communicates to us. The 'gift' promised to the disciples in Acts 1:4 (cf. 2:38; 8:20; 10:45; 11:17) is nothing else but God himself; the 'gift' is the 'giver'.

(2) The immanence of the Spirit is the immanence of God in his irreducible transcendence. That is, the God who is in our midst due to the donation of the Spirit (John 14:23; 1 Cor 14:25) is always Holy, he who is wholly other, the Lord whom even heaven cannot contain. In that context we dare not seek to make him our creature, or consider his presence as a partial

---

[32] For a fuller discussion, see my, 'The Spirit of the Father and the Spirit of the Son', 19–48.

[33] Torrance, *The Trinitarian Faith*, 191–251.

presence of God, but only act toward him in that holy fear characteristic of the angels. See Acts 5:4; 8:20; cf. Isa 66:1–2; Isa 6:1–5.

(3) The person of the Spirit is enhypostatic in the *being* (i.e. not the persons) of the Father and the Son. That is, in meeting the persons of the Trinity, and especially the Spirit, we are being directly met by the One True God. We are not being met at one level by the particularity of God to be led to his oneness or unity at a deeper level. If, however, the person of the Spirit was to arise in the 'persons' of the Father and the Son and not from their 'being', then God would not necessarily be in himself as he is towards us in the gospel. Knowledge of God in his inner being, if such knowledge were possible under these circumstances, would then have to lie somewhere qualitatively further on from the incarnation, the cross and Pentecost. See John 10:38; 17:1–5.

(4) 'The Spirit proceeds from the Father and receives from the Son' (Athanasius). We may with the Western creeds speak of 'the Spirit who proceeds from the Father and the Son', but we may not with some later theologians of the East say 'who proceeds from the Father, but *not* the Son'; for the Son is also fully God, and the fullness of the divinity of the Spirit shares in the fullness of the divinity of the Son. See John 14:15–27; 15:26; 16:5–15; 20:19–23.

(5) Only the Son is properly the 'image' of the Godhead made known, thus we only know the Spirit through the Son. See Colossians 1:15; 3:10; Hebrews 1:1–3.

Four corollaries for knowing God

These corollaries to the above statements are important, for on any definition, 'mission' has as its purpose the advancement of the knowledge of God, until 'the earth shall be full of the knowledge of the LORD as the waters cover the sea' (Isa 11:9; Exod 6:7; 7:5; 2 Cor 10:5).

(1) God may be known only from within himself. It was the great triumph of Athanasius and the creed of Nicaea-Constantinople to see from Holy Scripture that God

is so incomparable with anything we know, that it is not fitting for us to ask human questions about the Godhead. 'God may be known, not from without, but only from what he is within himself.'[34] In this respect, the person and work of the Spirit shows us that God is unconditionally and irreversibly Lord in his self revelation. See (1) and (2) above.

(2) The person and work (his indwelling of us) of the Spirit shows us that we can only think of the Holy Spirit dwelling in us by thinking of ourselves dwelling in God. In the words of Athanasius, 'the Holy Spirit is partaken but does not partake'.[35] He who is complete within himself does not receive from us, but we receive from him. The Holy Spirit is only ever the Spirit of God, never the spirit of humanity or the spirit of the age. The Hegelian structure of Moltmann's understanding of the person and operation of the Spirit is basically flawed. On the contrary, for us to know God we must be united to God through Christ in the Spirit, by faith, an insight fundamental to John Calvin. Not only is, in terms of the fathers, 'faith and godliness' (or 'piety' in John Calvin) necessary to the knowledge of God, but in this knowledge it is *God* we know, not some human construct or experience of the divine. See (1) and (2) above.

(3) The Spirit is not knowable in himself or approachable; he remains veiled behind the Father and the Son. The Spirit only presents himself amongst us in this transparent and translucent mode of being. See (3), (4), (5) above.

(4) But, the Holy Spirit, because of who he is and what he does, shows us that although God remains ineffable, he does not remain unintelligible. In the movement of the Spirit of the Father and the Son we have a real outward movement whereby God makes himself open to our knowing; *homoousion* shows us that we have a true movement of revelation of God's own intrinsic intelligibility (1 Cor 2:1–16, esp 10–11: 'the Spirit searches all things, even the deep things of God'). See (1), (2), (3), (4) above.

---

[34] Torrance, *The Trinitarian Faith*, 207.

[35] Torrance, *The Trinitarian Faith*, 209.

Consequences for thinking about mission

What I have attempted to do in the above is to outline the theological ground for mission, especially as it concerns pneumatology, that Scripture puts forward. This acts, in dialogue with the data of Scripture, to make sense of that data, and thus appropriately control our thinking as we exegete Scripture and place theological construction upon it. What then may we say by way of response to the questions raised by episcopal and pneumatological models of mission, and to the models themselves? I make the following observations:

(1) The doctrine of the Spirit confirms the insight that Tertullian was driven toward, that God does not operate indirectly in the world, but that in the sending and receiving of the Spirit we see that God is fully and personally present in his work. The notion that the three orders, and especially the bishop, is *the* sacrament of Christ and *the* channel of his work in the world is a fundamental denial of what God has promised. The mission is God's, and God is the missioner, and it is as the Spirit witnesses to Christ, that is, in the words of 1 Peter, the Spirit preaches the gospel (1 Pet 1:12), that God's kingdom is spread.

(2) The solution to the proper concern for *paradosis*, both with respect to its content and its handing on, lies in the fact that the Spirit is only present in his transparent and translucent mode of being. That is, he proceeds from the Father and receives from the Son in order to instruct the apostolic band as to the meaning of the life, teaching, death and resurrection of Jesus Christ. That *paradosis*, which not only instructs but also savingly illuminates the darkened human mind, the Church for some 1800 years has recognised to be contained in the canonical Scriptures, and has also, more or less, recognised that its handing on consists of the faithful teaching of the same Scriptures.

(3) The person and work of the Holy Spirit tells us that it is God in his holiness and transcendence who ordains people for mission. Our ordination can only appropriately follow after the fact, not precede it or control it. Further, because in the

Spirit we participate, or fellowship, in God's person and work, his concern for a recognisable and orderly public ministry is ours too. These are the leading ideas in Cranmer's ordinal. The launching of the Mission Department at Moore College is a divine necessity, not merely a human one.

(4) The truth that in the Spirit we actually partake or share or fellowship in the communion of the person and work of God not only destroys the false ontological necessity of the hierarchy inherent in the classical episcopal model of mission, but also reinforces the necessity for a connectivity and mutual responsibility between Christian congregations which is visible and apostolic. The one body we belong to in the Spirit is Christ (1 Cor 12:12–13 cf Eph 4:1–6). We are not free to disregard or shatter that unity. The doctrine of the Spirit's person and work tells us that the manner of unity is our sharing in the work of the Spirit, the preaching of Christ, the apostolic message about Christ. It is in this way that apostolic unity is expressed and nurtured, as we encourage, exhort, even rebuke each other in our attempts to understand and communicate the apostolic gospel. Someone who preaches the gospel beside me is not my competitor, but my co-worker, even if he or she should do it with base motive, for it is Christ whom we and the Spirit preach (Phil 1:15–18).

(5) Because he is the one who in his residence spreads the love of God abroad in our hearts (Rom 5:5), the Spirit may be described as the mutual love between the Father and the Son, or at the very least, the one who brings God, who is love, into the very centre of our being. It is thus fitting in our ordination in the Spirit for mission that we love one another in our mutual participation in that mission (1 Cor 14:1). That mutual love in mission is primarily expressed in recognition of the divine validity of the other's proclamation. This is not a submission to a human *episkopos*, but to the Lord who is the Spirit.

(6) The fact that in the Spirit we participate in the mission of God means that the relation between a missioner and a bishop, to whom we by human agreement have given the responsibility to act as a Timothy to inquire about and promote apostolic concerns in our mission, changes the

emphasis in the old formula: 'Receive this charge which is yours and mine.' 'This charge' is the Spirit's; 'yours and mine' means partnership, not jurisdiction.

(7) That the Spirit is the Spirit of the Father and the Son means that there is no qualitative gap between the cross and Pentecost. The gifts the Spirit distributes are for the ministry of the proclamation of the gospel of Christ, are the gifts of Christ, and are distributed sovereignly. The gifts that we actually have are sufficient, for that is the promise. Our task is to earnestly desire to prophesy, the content of which is the gospel, the message of Christ. That is the only soil from which mission appropriately springs, and it is a given. In the possession of the gifts, we do not have a sacramental precondition through which God works, but the actual direct working of God now. If we especially see an unction of the transparent and translucent Spirit in this, it ought be because of the presence of the message about Christ, not because of the presence or absence of eye-catching phenomena.

(8) Because the Spirit is God himself present in our midst making himself known as he truly is in himself as Father, Son and Holy Spirit, then we may not expect the Spirit to be revealing the one true God in other, non-Christian religions. In the light of the knowledge of God which we see in the face of Jesus Christ, the Spirit calls upon all the religions to do exactly what the religion of Christendom must do, 'repent, and believe the gospel'. Because God is both content and Lord of his own self-revelation, we cannot expect to build from human constructs to knowledge of God, even religious constructs, which Israel also must acknowledge (Rom 3:9–31 cf. Rom 9 to 11).

(9) The sovereign freedom of the Spirit in his revelation of God is the sovereign freedom of the Spirit of *God*. He reveals only God, only the Father and the Son, and in this way only himself, through the apostolic gospel. The 'Gamaliel principle' arises in the NT in terms of how and to what extent the preaching of the apostles about Christ was in continuity with God's plans for Israel. By the end of the book of Acts, the answer has come as a resounding 'yes'—it is in continuity, even if some in Israel will not hear it. To seek to apply 'the

Gamaliel' principle today is to enter deeply into the unbelief of Israel. When we observe freelance work proceeding, that is, work which preaches Christ, our question ought not be whether this is the work of God, but rather, how may we be partners in this work.

Exploring further

1. How does the book of Acts relate together the themes of 'word' and 'Spirit'?
2. Describe and assess the place given by the Book of Common Prayer to the person and work of the Holy Spirit.
3. From the point of view of the New Testament, what place and role may we give our post apostolic understanding of episcopacy?
4. How does the New Testament understand 'gifts' for ministry and their relationship to our participation in the mission of God?

4

Obstacles and Opportunities

Phillip Jensen

Synopsis

Much of the literature that discusses contemporary obstacles to and opportunities for Christian mission suffers from the confusion of anthropology and theology. This confusion can be traced back to Feuerbach who claimed that the knowledge of God is really just the knowledge of humanity. This is a half truth. Since God has created a habitable world in his wisdom, wisdom can be derived from observations of God's world. The Church Growth movement represents an attempt to do this by applying insights from sociology to the work of planting and building Christian congregations. Unfortunately, church growth literature also illustrates the lie of anthropology-as-theology. The writings of the Canadian humanist, John Ralston Saul, show how corrupt dictators have employed the efficiencies of technology to foster their tyranny. A similar technology-as-ideology can be detected in church growth literature. Once church growth technology is detached from a gospel framework any religious group can employ it to build their organisation. The obstacles and opportunities for mission must be discussed within a theological framework. The paper proposes such a framework under six headings—God's sovereign rule, God's timing, the nature of the gospel, God's co-workers, human nature and Satan's opposition. There is a place for anthropology in preparing for mission, but it must be theological anthropology. Having understood the task in the light of God's revelation, we will be committed to the prayerful, faithful presentation of God's word, trusting him for the spiritual work of regeneration.

Theology and anthropology

During the 1960's I began as a student of geography at Sydney University. Naturally I was eager to find out what geography involved. After the initial confusion, a few defining characteristics emerged. Basically, geography was what geographers did and like most other disciplines within the humanities, geography was the study of everything. Even more importantly, being the 1960's, geography was a science. This was the great path to legitimacy, for any discipline, at that time. Since those days science has fallen out of fashion a little, no longer invoked with the same enthusiasm.

There was another fashion prevalent at the time, whose influence has continued and shows little sign of abating. This is the belief that theology is really just a branch of anthropology. In other words, Feuerbach has won. The eighteenth century German philosopher maintained that 'the knowledge of God (is) nothing else than a knowledge of man!'[1] The dictum has won wide acceptance and had extensive influence. According to Noll, here is the root of Marx's view of religion as an opiate. Here too is a root of Freud's view of religion as an illusion.[2] And here is the resting place for George Eliot's views about religion.

---

[1] L. A. Feuerbach, *The Essence of Christianity* (Tr. G. Eliot; New York: Harper, 1957) 207, 'between the divine revelation and the so-called human reason or nature, there is no other than an illusory distinction; the contents of the divine revelation are of human origin, for they have proceeded not from God as God, but from God as determined by human reason, human wants, that is, directly from human reason and human wants. And so in revelation man goes out of himself, in order, by a circuitous path, to return to himself! Here we have a striking confirmation of the position that the secret of theology is nothing else than anthropology—the knowledge of God nothing else than a knowledge of man!'

[2] M. A. Noll, 'Feuerbach, Ludwig Andreas' in S. B. Ferguson and D. F. Wright, eds. *New Dictionary of Theology* (Leicester: IVP, 1988) 259, 'Feuerbach's ideas had a significant influence on Karl Marx and Friedrich Engels who drew from him the belief that the material realm is the basis for all ideology. For Marx, Feuerbach established true materialism and true science by demonstrating that human social experience establishes our conception of humankind.'

Feuerbach's definition of theology has continued to reverberate into our century. It was in the early 1960's that J. A. T. Robinson endorsed the perspective in his book, *Honest to God*. According to Robinson, 'Feuerbach was right in wanting to translate "theology" into "anthropology".'[3] It was an opinion fully shared by another influential German of this century, Rudolf Bultmann, who said 'I would heartily agree: I *am* trying to substitute anthropology for theology, for I am interpreting theological affirmations as assertions about human life'.[4]

Wisdom in God's world

The reduction of theology to anthropology without remainder is a lie. However, like any successful lie, its appeal comes from the half-truth it contains. Lies like this would not deceive if they did not contain some element of truth. The lie that got us all into our present mess claimed that Adam and Eve would become like God once they ate the fruit from the tree of knowledge of good and evil (Gen 3:5). That it contained some truth is confirmed after they swallow the lie, when God says: 'See, the man has become like one of us, knowing good and evil' (Gen 3:22).

Similarly, the lie that theology is anthropology contains a half-truth. Certainly, much bad theology is just anthropology, with horizons limited to the history of religions or the psychology of religion. Religion is confined then to the human search for God. Feuerbach's followers have made sure of that. However, even good theology will recognise the place of careful observation of human activity and the created order. God in his wisdom placed the man and woman over a habitable world to subdue and rule over it in his image. Even in the chaotic world after Adam's rebellion, humanity is called to live by the wisdom that is reflected in God's world.

---

[3] J. A. T. Robinson, *Honest to God* (London: SCM, 1963) 50, 'If statements about God are statements about the "ultimacy" of personal relationships, then we must agree in a real sense Feuerbach was right in wanting to translate "theology" into "anthropology". He was concerned to restore the divine attributes from heaven to earth, whence, he believed, they had been filched and projected on to a perfect Being, an imaginary Subject before whom impoverished man falls in worship.'

[4] Cited in Robinson, 50.

So, the great wise man, Solomon, studied and taught botany and zoology. His wisdom was universally acknowledged as greater than that of the East and the Egyptians. Such a comparison implies that Solomon's was a similar wisdom to their wisdom. According to 1 Kings:

> God gave Solomon very great wisdom, discernment, and breadth of understanding as vast as the sand on the seashore, so that Solomon's wisdom surpassed the wisdom of all the people of the east, and all the wisdom of Egypt. He was wiser than anyone else, wiser than Ethan the Ezrahite, and Heman, Calcol and Darda, children of Mahol; his fame spread throughout all the surrounding nations. He composed three thousand proverbs, and his songs numbered a thousand and five. He would speak of trees, from the cedar that is in the Lebanon to the hyssop that grows in the wall; he would speak of animals, and birds, and reptiles and fish. People came from all the nations to hear the wisdom of Solomon; they came from all the kings of the earth who had heard of his wisdom. (1 Kings 4:29–34)

In keeping with this description, Solomon's proverbs report the wisdom observed in the world around him. Proverbs 6:6 urges the sluggard to go to the ant and 'consider its ways, and be wise'. The ants, along with badgers and locusts and lizards of God's world, have their share of wisdom:

> Four things on earth are small,
> yet they are exceedingly wise:
> the ants are a people without strength,
> yet they provide their food in the summer;
> the badgers are a people without power,
> yet they make their homes in the rocks;
> the locusts have no king,
> yet all of them march in rank;
> the lizard can be grasped in the hand,
> yet it is found in kings' palaces. (Prov 30:24–28)

Thus it is, by careful observation, that we can learn from this world about the ways of wisdom and the ways of God.

The same principle can equally be illustrated from the NT. Paul urges Timothy:

> Share in suffering like a good soldier of Christ Jesus. No one serving in the army gets entangled in everyday affairs; the soldier's aim is to please the enlisting officer. And in the case of an athlete, no one is crowned without competing according to the rules. It is the farmer who does the work who ought to have the first share of the crops. Think over what I say, for the Lord will give you understanding in all things. (2 Tim 2:3–7)

As Timothy carries out 'the work of an evangelist' (2 Tim 4:5), Paul's is not the only example to learn from (2 Tim 3:10,11). Even the soldier, the athlete and the farmer operate within a wisdom that can be understood and applied to gospel ministry.

The Church Growth Movement

It is against this background that the Church Growth Movement has arisen and is best understood. As a missionary in India, Donald McGavran observed the enormous number of missionaries around him. He also witnessed the enormous effort being expended in preaching, teaching, caring and feeding the hungry. Yet his observations told him that few people were being won for Christ and churches were failing to grow.

So McGavran set out on a quest to analyse why churches do not grow and to discover how growth might be stimulated. In 1961 he established the North West Christian College in Eugene, Oregon. In 1965 he became the founding Dean of Fuller Theological Seminary Graduate School of Mission. The lessons learnt from the mission field were applied systematically to churches in North America. Since then the whole methodological discipline of church growth has spread throughout the world.

The important thing to note about McGavran was that he had previously moved from liberalism to evangelicalism. So under his leadership, the Church Growth Movement was driven by a passion for the salvation of the lost by evangelism, as this extract illustrates:

> After declaring that he has become all things to all men that he might save some, the apostle Paul says, 'Be imitators of me as I am of Christ.' Denying oneself and making every effort to save men and women is essential Christian behavior . . .
>
> True, the growth of the church will produce more members. They will give more, build more beautiful sanctuaries, and pay their ministers more. But none of these are good reasons for church growth. The good reasons are Christ's commands and example to seek and save the lost. While Christians are properly concerned with the physical man, the Bible is clear that salvation is an infinitely greater good than a full belly or a warm bed. The Church Growth Movement is driven by a conviction that heaven, even if to get there entails being eaten by lions in the Colosseum, is preferable to hell after living a comfortable life.
>
> Furthermore, the Bible is clear that if we want brotherhood, equality, and justice in the world, there is no surer way of getting it than to lead multitudes to become spirit-filled followers of Jesus Christ. The kingdom of God is not an ethical paradise in which men of every philosophy and shade of opinion gather. The kingdom of God first and foremost is that nation in which all citizens believe in Jesus Christ the King. As a result, the kingdom exhibits far more kindness, mercy, justice, and brotherhood than any association of unconverted men and women. Multitudes must become followers of Christ.[5]

The theological conservativism of its founder meant the Church Growth Movement began as the study of methods to grow churches within the context of a gospel mindset. With brutal honesty it looked to the real facts of churches' growth and non-growth. It applied statistical methodology. It used marketing strategies. It created a new vocabulary; terms like 'homogenous unit principle', 'winnable people', 'people groups' and 'contextualisation'.

---

[5] D. A. McGavran, 'Church Growth Movement' in W. A. Elwell, ed., *Evangelical Dictionary of Theology* (Grand Rapids: Baker, 1984) 241.

In the process it adopted a variety of research methods, business techniques and principles from secular sociological studies. These were carefully applied to the planting, organisation and management of churches. They were also applied to the way ministry and a minister's role were understood. In other words, anthropology was applied to church.

You may remember that earlier in this paper I suggested that theology as anthropology was only half true. That means it is also half false. Though we can live wisely in God's wise world, it is fear of the Lord that is the beginning of wisdom. The wisdom of the world that is lived in hostility, defiance and rebellion against God is a distorted and perverted wisdom.

McGavran had a clear conversion out of liberalism into evangelicalism. Consequently the methods he developed were developed to promote evangelicalism. However, his disciples, proteges and successors were more committed to church growth and his methodology than to evangelicalism.

As a result, McGavran's goals and principles were taken from their context. The mechanisms of church growth like parking lot capacity, modern music, contemporary advertising methods and a clear simple message, have been detached from the paradigm of explicitly evangelical ministry and attached to any and every religious group that wishes to grow. This exposes the fact that ultimately these mechanisms do not arise out of gospel theology but out of humanistic anthropology.

The Harvard School of Business Administration

An unexpected and interesting insight into this phenomenon is gained through the writings of John Ralston Saul. Saul is a Canadian humanist who writes as a historian, novelist, businessman, social commentator and media guru. He traces a number of key themes of twentieth–century history to the Enlightenment. Saul's analysis[6] of our present social scene might be summarised like this:

[6] J. R. Saul, *Voltaire's Bastards. The Dictatorship of Reason in the West* (Toronto: Penguin, 1993).

1. Voltaire and other thinkers of the eighteenth century attacked the idea of government by entrenched power of aristocracy and church.
2. Voltaire and his friends argued for rational government, informed by reason alone.
3. However, John Ralston Saul argues that reason alone is inhuman and inadequate for it lacks purpose and morality (amongst other things). Over time it is inevitably reduced to technology.
4. The classic training in this 'reason alone' technology is that created by the time and motion engineer, Frederick Winslow Taylor. Taylor's thinking gave rise to the Harvard School of Business Administration. This 'reason alone' technology not only spawned M.B.A. programs all over the world but also amoral, purposeless, long-term devastating, inhumane managers, technicians, quick-fix bureaucrats and corporate planners.
5. So we now have better bombs and armaments, manufactured with greater speed, accuracy and efficiency, used as a basis for our economic growth and the provision of employment. It is all corporately hyper-efficient but also profoundly, deeply inhuman, misdirected and stupid.
6. John Ralston Saul sees Napoleon, Hitler, Stalin and Mussolini as illegitimate but true offspring of Voltaire's rationality. The last three used Harvard Business Administration graduates to create their particular nightmares.

The church growth movement seems a long way from Napoleon, Hitler, Stalin and Mussolini. However, the commitment to technology over ideology or to technology as ideology is in fact the same. The Harvard M.B.A. is still at the base of the curriculum. So as you read church growth literature you will notice no consensus about 'what is the gospel?' or 'what is the church?' In fact you will not find any real definition or discussion of the nature of the gospel or the nature of church.

Church growth is about how to grow your church, whatever your church is. Church growth is about how to grow your church whatever gospel it preaches. And the only gospel of church growth is that churches should grow.

Obstacles and opportunities

All of this has been a long explanatory introduction to the topic of 'Obstacles and Opportunities'. As we turn to consider the nature of Christian mission, and prepare ourselves for the challenges we will meet, we must avoid the trap of confusing anthropology with theology. Because there is some truth in anthropology, even secular anthropology, we are easily seduced into thinking that the truth about contemporary mission is found there. However, truth lies not in the study of humanity, but in the truth of God.

If we are to see the fields 'white unto harvest' then we must look with theological eyes, not with a sociological, anthropological and humanistic vision. The details of the what and where of obstacles and opportunities are not important. The basis from which we assess them is everything. So in the remaining material I want to outline six topics that provide the theological perspective from which obstacles and opportunities are seen for what they are.

God

To understand mission we have to understand God and the way he rules his world. The mission we are engaged in is God's mission; we are his fellow workers (2 Cor 6:1; 1 Thess 3:2); we are doing the work of the Lord (1 Cor 15:58; 16:10); he is the sovereign ruler over all creation, right down to the heart which he can direct wherever he likes (Prov 21:1). As a result, we know that God provides obstacles and opportunities according to his will. Likewise, we know that he removes obstacles and opportunities according to his good purpose.

The NT constantly reminds us that the mission is God's. Paul is prevented from preaching in Asia by the Holy Spirit (Acts 16:6) and in Bythinia by the Spirit of Christ (Acts 16:7). God led Paul in triumphal procession (2 Cor 2:14), appointed those who believed in Pisidian Antioch to eternal life (Acts 13:48), granted repentance to the Gentiles (Acts 11:13), and purified the hearts of Gentiles (Acts 15:7,8). It was the Lord who opened Lydia's heart (Acts 16:14) and insisted that Paul continue to speak because he had many people in Corinth (Acts 18:9,10).

Paul never lost sight of this fact. The apostle urges his readers to pray that 'the word of the Lord may spread rapidly and be glorified everywhere' (2 Thess 3:1). Note the way he interprets the positive response of people to his message. Their faith becomes the occasion of prayer and thanks. As he reflects on the conversion of the Thessalonians, he recognises who stood behind it:

> we also constantly give thanks to God for this, that when you received the word of God . . . you accepted it not as a human word, but as it really is, God's word, which is also at work in you believers. (1 Thess 2:13)

Just as the prospectors keep digging because they know there is gold in the ground, so evangelists keep preaching because they know that God is calling his people by the gospel. Whenever we engage in evangelism we will be reminded of the fact. Recently I heard of a girl who, having been converted at a mission, asked her friend to come along with her to the next meeting. Her friend was so thrilled to hear the OT expounded that she invited other non-Christian friends to attend the mission. That only happens because God is at work.

Timing

The mission is God's and proceeds according to his plan and purposes. He has revealed his plan and purposes in his word so that we can know where we are up to in his timing. Unless we are conscious of carrying out God's mission in the last days we will never understand the task.

Some years ago, on the basis of Matthew 28:19,20, a doctor applied to the Church Missionary Society with a view to using his skills as a medical practitioner overseas. In order to prepare he enrolled in the one year 'Bible and Mission' course at Moore College. During the course he encountered biblical theology for the first time, he began to comprehend God's great plan of salvation and he understood God's perspective on the period of history in which he was living

As a result he saw that Matthew 28:19,20 was more than just the eleventh commandment. He realised that there was more to mission than practising medicine overseas. He saw that there was more to theology than completing a one year course so as to gain theological accreditation. He recognised that according to God's timetable it was time to preach God's word to God's world.

We must understand biblical eschatology aright if we are going to see obstacles and opportunities clearly. By biblical eschatology I do not mean the use of biblical phrases like 'the day of small things' to rationalise our lack of urgency and our failure. Rather our whole outlook on life, ministry and mission needs to be informed by the Bible's account of the times in which we live.

For 'now is the day of salvation' (2 Cor 6:2). Now is the kingdom come and yet to come. Now is the time for the gentiles (Luke 21:24). Now the times when God overlooked ignorance have come to an end. Now we have the resurrection as evidence of the day of judgment that has been fixed, when God will judge the world with justice (Acts 17:30, 31). Now is the time for repentance, thanks to the patience of God (2 Pet 3:9).

Dispense with this eschatological plan of God and the opportunities and obstacles for mission disappear as surely as the mission itself evaporates. With an understanding of eschatology we will look for and recognise the obstacles characteristic of the last days when people will not put up with sound doctrine (2 Tim 3:1; 4:3). We will discern the dragon making war against those who obey God's commandments and hold to the testimony of Jesus (Rev 12:13–17). We will also ignore the seasonality of human affairs because we preach the word in the presence of God and of Christ Jesus who will judge the living and the dead, and in view of his appearing and his kingdom (2 Tim 4:1).

Gospel

The gospel itself generates obstacles and opportunities for those who preach. They will encounter both because the word of God is powerful, active, dynamic and living (Ps 33:6; Heb 4:12,13), because the gospel is bearing fruit and growing (Col 1:6), because the word sown multiplies thirty, sixty and one hundredfold (Mark 4:20), and because the gospel is the power of God to salvation (Rom 1:16; 1 Cor 1:18).

So the gospel creates opportunities. It is the nature of the message that accounts for the fact the apostles were the aroma of Christ, the sweet fragrance of life to those who were saved (2 Cor 2:14–16). It means we will experience the joy of witnessing lives transformed by the message we preach, people turning from their idols to serve the living God (1 Thess 1:9, 10).

At the same time, the gospel is the source of a variety of obstacles. We must not forget that the apostles were also a pungent odour of death to those who were perishing (2 Cor 2:14–16). The gospel will bring us persecution, and with it bring the temptation to be ashamed to testify about the Lord, ashamed of Paul and ashamed of the message itself (2 Tim 1:8). We are called to share in the suffering involved in faithfully guarding the good deposit and transmitting it. We must pray for fearlessness to make known the salvation of all by the gospel in the face of all kinds of obstacles.

Us

It is in the face of these circumstances that we create opportunities for and obstacles to the mission. This is true because of choices God has made. He chose to use humans as his fellow workers and the foolishness of what we preach (1 Cor 1:18). God chose to use jars of clay to demonstrate the power of his message (2 Cor 4:7). He ordained that the praises of God should come from the mouths of babes and little children (Ps 8:2). God has chosen to use us—his people.

He did not have to make these choices. He could write on walls (Daniel 5). He could speak by donkeys (Num 22:28). He could have sent his angels. However he chose to give his gifts to us. He distributed many gifts to all and sundry, just as he pleased, in order for his church to be built (Eph 4:7–16). This means many, many opportunities to participate in God's mission.

Yet, since our sinfulness continues to plague us, we present some of the obstacles to that mission. Some are lazy in using our gifts. We take pride in ourselves rather than boasting of the Lord. Many of us seek fulfilment and spiritual standing through our gifts. Some will even try to use them to make money, instead of serving him.

So instead of following the examples of Christ and of Paul in laying down our lives for the salvation of others, we distort the truth to draw away our own disciples. Or we lord it over the flock, greedy for money (1 Pet 5:2,3). We do not 'proclaim Christ as Lord, and ourselves as your slaves for Jesus' sake' (2 Cor 4:5) but proclaim ourselves and expect the congregation to serve us.

We refuse to deny ourselves, take up our cross and follow Jesus (Mark 8:34), insisting instead on having a foxhole and a birdnest (4 bedrooms, study, 1.5 bathrooms, family, lounge and dining). Too often our eyes stare back at the world as we put our hand to the plough (Luke 9:62). As a consequence, the mission is hampered, because we lose sight of the kingdom of God and seek to build our own, individual kingdoms.

Even when we gather together in his name, the way we fellowship together in church frequently proves a source of obstacles to the mission. We have allowed technology and anthropology to dictate the nature of our meetings. Seeker services are shaped by our perception of the felt needs of the audience. Beginning with 'where are people itching?', rather than the gospel, may yield some short term gain, but in the long term it will be a disaster.

Too many contemporary songs leave us singing all about 'us' and our commitment rather than God, Jesus and the great theological truths of the gospel. Group Bible study resources are so intent on 'relevant' application they focus on our preoccupations rather than the Bible's. Similarly, as Anglican congregations move away from the Prayer Book many are trying to fill the vacuum with packages that have worked in other contexts. Buying packages off the shelf is dangerous. If they are not faithful to biblical and Anglican values then we introduce a virus into our computer.

That is not to say we will not engage with people and the matters that concern them most. However we must not confuse 'scratching where they are itching' with the gospel. It is one thing to begin a talk with where people are at, but it is quite another to go out and ask what people are thinking in order to work out what we should say to them. Inevitably, if we are going to communicate, we will engage in anthropology, but it must be theological anthropology.

People

The people of this world present their obstacles and opportunities for mission, but not as the world and secular anthropology would suggest. It is not that certain classes, groups, psychological types, cultures, nations or age-groups are more winnable than others or ought to be our special focus. There are certain people who may be more reachable with our message because of distance, language or culture. But no-one has greater claim upon our preaching than anyone else, with the possible exception of the Jews (Rom 1:16).

If the Bible is informing our mission, then our expectation will be that no-one is searching after the one, true and living God. Though all will know of him, all will be idolatrously rebellious against him. All people try to suppress the truth of him, in order to continue in their sinfulness (Rom 1:18–21). Only by the regenerating work of the Spirit will we see people pressing into the kingdom, desiring to know God.

Thus we will always encounter the obstacles erected by intellectual rationalisation as we preach the gospel. We will meet the murderous lies of the father of lies (John 8:44) which lead people to seek human glory rather than God's. Instead of believing the truth people will be readily impressed by counterfeit miracles, powerful experiences and clever rhetoric.

Confronting people with the gospel as we engage in mission will require us to remove the intellectual fortresses behind which sinners hide from the light so that their culpability is not exposed. Once the fortress is demolished they are likely to scurry away from the light again to find another bogus fortress of falsehood and fear. We cannot argue people into the kingdom.

Jesus said 'If they do not listen to Moses and the prophets, neither will they be convinced even if someone rises from the dead' (Luke 16:31). Neither the miraculous sign nor the apologetic argument will convince the unregenerate. Jesus also said, 'My sheep listen to my voice; I know them, and they follow me' (John 10:27). Nowhere is this more clearly illustrated than in the Pharisees' response to Jesus:

> And all the people who heard this, including the tax collectors, acknowledged the justice of God, because they had been baptised with John's baptism. But by refusing to be baptised by him, the Pharisees and the lawyers rejected God's purpose for themselves. (Luke 7:29, 30)

Our task is to do God's work by faithfully reaching whoever is reachable with the word of God. We know that God is at work bringing his people to himself through our activity. People who respond to God's mercy create opportunities. Those who reject God's mercy create obstacles.

Satan

There is one other dimension to the obstacles and opportunities anyone involved in God's mission will encounter. That is Satan. There is cosmic opposition to God, from one who is not equal to God, and who is used by God in the accomplishment of his purposes. This means that even the obstacles the evil one places in our path can be opportunities for God to display his grace. So the thorn in the flesh from Satan becomes a way of keeping Paul from conceitedness (2 Cor 12:7–10).

Satan works by placing obstacles in our paths (1 Thess 2:18), tempting young converts (1 Cor 7:5) and roaming around seeking victims to devour (1 Pet 5:8). For, as Paul points out,

> our struggle is not against enemies of blood and flesh, but against the rulers, against the authorities, against the cosmic powers of this present darkness, against the spiritual forces of evil in the heavenly places. (Eph 6:12)

Therefore the weapons we have been given to enter into the conflict with are 'not weapons of the world' (2 Cor 10:4). Our armour consists of the blessings of the gospel. Our sword is the word of God (Eph 6:13–17).

Theological anthropology

If we are to gain true insight into the opportunities for, and obstacles to mission we will need to turn away from the seductive appeal of anthropology-as-theology and technology-as-ideology. Our faith is in God and his word, not sociology and its findings. This is not meant to imply that there is no place for anthropology. Rather it is to seek to work out a *theological* anthropology instead of an atheological one, which will inevitably become an antitheological anthropology.

How to communicate the truth

From the vantage point of a truly theological anthropology we can begin to answer the question of how to communicate the truth. The Bible and atheists like Samuel Beckett and David Hume would agree that without God we have the epistemological nihilism of postmodernism. The Bible and atheists like Sartre and Nietszche would agree that without God we have the moral vacuum of postmodern Western society.

How can we communicate the truth to a rebellious world that suppresses the truth? Our temptation is to use the world's technology, not to reach the reachable with the word of God, but to win the winnable to our church. So we have all kinds of method evangelism including conferences like Cursillo, dinners like Alpha, conventions like Promise Keepers, crusades like Billy Graham's, discipling methods like Navigators, meetings like seeker services and presentations like *Two Ways to Live*. We fail to communicate the truth when we rely on the methods rather than the message they were designed to serve.

However the work of the mission of Christ is carried out by prayerful, faithful presentation of God's word, blessed by the Spirit's work of regeneration. Is it simply foolish and weak? It has always seemed that way. But no, in God's mercy, it is wise and strong. We must not lose confidence in our message.

Obstacles and opportunities

Once we have resolved how to communicate in the light of this theological anthropology, we are then in a position to see the opportunities we have by virtue of our wealth, our political liberty and peace, our education, our mobility, our access to the media and the fact that our first language is English. Then we will be able to see more clearly the obstacles that are provided by our deadening, cultural religion, our domestication by society and our endless divisions over secondary matters.

While an analysis of these factors would be worthy of further examination, it would take another paper; perhaps the paper I was meant to give. Yet these further considerations are a mere footnote to the larger issue I have tried to address.

If we are to discuss obstacles and opportunities for mission as the millennium comes to a close, then we must do so from the vantage point of the gospel.

Exploring further

1. In the light of the theological framework offered in this paper, why would people find Feuerbach's reduction of theology to anthroplogy attractive?
2. What positive use of human wisdom can Christians make? Of what value is the wisdom literature of the OT to living the Christian life?
3. How should an awareness of living in the last days affect the way we approach evangelism?
4. What impact does human sinfulness have on mission in terms of:
    a. those who preach the gospel?
    b. those to whom the gospel is preached?
5. What happens when we underestimate the deceitfulness of the human heart?
6. What encouragement is there in the sovereignty of God as we seek to carry out the mission entrusted to us?

5

'Sent For This Purpose': 'Mission' and 'Missiology' and their Search for Meaning

Michael Raiter

Synopsis

There is widespread confusion about the meaning of the term 'mission'. Most writings on the topic begin with an assumed, but unsubstantiated, understanding of mission. In order to grapple with important missiological issues we need to be clear what the word is pointing to. That can only happen by establishing a firm methodology for exploring a definition of mission. Such a methodology must start with an investigation into the key term to which 'mission' is related—'sending.'

The NT evidence is that God sends his Son, his Spirit, and his servants for one unified salvific purpose: to proclaim the gospel so that churches can be established and be brought to maturity on the day of Christ. This is consistent with God's purposes for his creation as found in the Bible's metanarrative. In short, God draws people out of tribe, people, and tongue that they might come to Christ and worship the triune God.

This understanding of mission gives us the necessary framework for exploring such important contemporary issues as the relationship between verbal proclamation and works of compassion, the scope of mission and whether mission demands that one 'go' elsewhere in order to do this work. This framework also helps to set the parameters for the study of missiology which must be rescued from its captivity to the social sciences and returned to its proper moorings in biblical studies and Christian thought.

Defining 'Mission'

It was twenty years ago that, returning home from teaching my classes at a local high school, I phoned my mother and told her that I had just decided to become a missionary. This was the first time I had mentioned anything like this to my parents and yet, instinctively, she understood by the word 'missionary' that her son would soon leave Australia for a foreign land. The term 'missionary' immediately conjures up in people's minds the image of the cross-cultural worker ministering overseas. Interestingly, in common usage the related term 'mission' does not carry this same connotation. Consider these other statements: 'Next week I'm off to Canberra for our annual college mission'; or 'Our local church is planning a mission this year'; or again, 'My mission in life is to help the runaway kids on our streets.'

All of these statements are commonly understood and accepted uses of the word 'mission'. If you announce that you have decided to become a missionary the immediate response this would elicit is, 'Really, so what country are you going to?' If you announce that you are embarking on a 'mission' you may be staying at home, going a short distance, or travelling to a different culture; only the context will tell your hearer the location of your mission. Similarly, the terms 'mission' and 'missionary' do not really indicate the character of the work that you will be engaging in. Within evangelical circles the announcement of a church's forthcoming 'mission' implies an evangelistic endeavour aimed at bringing the gospel to those outside the church. However, should someone decide to 'become a missionary' then they could be embarking on almost any kind of work from Bible translation to computer programming, from physiotherapy to teaching high school science. In the same vein, a Christian could legitimately describe his dedication to any non-evangelistic enterprise as their 'mission in life'.

When we survey what is happening in the world in the name of Christ under the rubric 'mission', then we encounter such a bewildering array of activities that we may end up with a definition of mission similar to the one which John Stott has given. For Stott 'mission' describes 'every act of service which God sends his redeemed people into the world to do'.[1] All of this can be confusing to the average Christian. If mission is everything which the church is sent into the world to do, and I am serving here in my little corner of the world, then I (along with every other believer) am a missionary. Mission director, David Porter, said this very thing in an article published in 1990. He wrote, 'Most Christians will remain ordinary disciples in ordinary jobs, with routine lives and it is to these that the task of missions is given'.[2] Porter is reflecting Stott's understanding of mission, as every act of service, no matter how ordinary and mundane, done in the name of Christ. Therefore, Porter argues, we ought to dispense with the word 'missionary' 'because every disciple of Jesus, by definition, is to be concerned with mission'. 'Missionary' then, is just a synonym for 'Christian servant'. So, if we are all missionaries wherever we are doing, then there is no need to go 'over there' when I can be a missionary right here. Further, if a missionary is a Christian servant and all God's people are by definition 'missionaries', why is Moore College establishing a Department of 'Mission'? We already have a Department of 'Ministry' in the college and, if Stott is to be followed, then ministry / servanthood and mission are really coterminous and so this new department, over whose establishment there has been so much excitement, appears superfluous!

In other words what, if anything, is distinctive about 'mission'? Our first task must be an attempt at a definition of 'mission' that is true to Scripture. Of course the exercise of constructing any such definition is never conducted in a theological vacuum. The context of this discussion will be, firstly, the contemporary understanding of mission as articulated by Stott, and now widely accepted. In short, is a proper understanding of 'mission' exclusive, focussing only on those

---

[1] J. Stott, *Christian Mission in the Modern World* (London: Falcon, 1975) 30.

[2] D. Porter, 'The New Christian', *Go*, July–September, 1990, 13.

ministries related to verbal gospel proclamation, or is it inclusive, embracing the many acts of loving service performed by God's people for the sake of Christ? Secondly, and following on from this first point, is 'mission' only over there, or does it include tasks God has given us on our doorstep?

In the light of our findings we will then attempt a definition of 'missiology'. The study of this comparatively new science (although it is much older than most recognise) is the purpose of our newly established Department of Mission and so it is appropriate that we clearly delineate the parameters of this study and then ask ourselves what is the particular contribution that Moore College can make to the study of mission.

What is 'Mission'?

In the ever-enlarging (but as yet unpublished) *Dictionary of Slippery Terms*, along with established banana skins like 'gospel', 'evangelical', and 'inerrant', the term 'mission' deserves pride of place. As with these other terms, it has only been in this century that a word which once held a clear and circumscribed definition has become so broadened in meaning that now it cannot stand on its own, but requires precise qualification by the author in order for the reader to understand what is meant by the word.

The term 'mission' (from the Latin *missio*, 'to send') was first coined by the Jesuits to describe the propagation of the Catholic faith amongst those (including Protestants) who were not members of the Catholic Church. Historically it was understood as the propagation of Christianity, although very often westernisation of the heathen went hand in hand with their Christianisation. Today the emphasis has shifted from that human activity of propagation or evangelisation to an emphasis on the *missio dei;* the recognition that mission is primarily God's mission and all that we do emanates from the prior sending of the Son by the Father. Still, there is considerable divergence of opinion over what kinds of work 'mission' entails. David Bosch, after an extensive examination of two thousand years of Christian missions and an investigation into the contemporary 'paradigm shift' in thinking about the meaning of mission, concludes that the term defies precise definition. 'And yet', he writes, 'even the attempt to list some of the dimensions of mission is fraught with danger, because it again suggests that we can define the infinite.'[3]

The problem of methodology

Given that 'mission' is not a word found in the Scriptures we immediately have a problem of methodology. How does one establish a biblical theology of mission? While, for example, there is a wide variety of understanding of what 'salvation' is, at least we can agree on a biblical word group (*sōter/sōtērion)* which can regulate our investigation. What do we do with a term not found in the Scriptures? Commonly an approach might be to begin with a preliminary definition of mission and then, in the light of that definition, examine all examples of that activity in the Scriptures. But how can one know that one's definition, which has become the grid for reading all the imagined relevant texts, is reliable? Alternatively, one may decide to withhold a definition of mission until one has examined all the evidence, and in the light of one's survey formulate a definition of mission. The difficulty of this approach is even more obvious; how does one discern which of the biblical evidence is relevant to mission unless one is already working with a presumed definition in the first place. Much of modern writing in mission falters because it has not established an appropriate methodology.

The way to proceed must be to begin with the word itself. We have already noted that historically the term means literally 'to send'. Many contemporary definitions of mission recognise this element of sending as being integral to the term (e.g. Stott's). While it would be reductionistic to limit one's study to the 'sending' word group in the Scriptures, and one ought to also study other terms which speak of 'movement' (e.g. coming, going, etc.), nevertheless an etymological and thematic study of 'sending' in the Scriptures must be the starting point for an investigation into mission. Consequently, this paper will begin with a brief overview of 'sending' in the NT. I am all too aware of

---

[3] D. Bosch, *Transforming Mission: Paradigm Shifts in Theology of Mission* (Maryknoll: Orbis, 1991) 512.

the limits of this approach; that one cannot assume the full meaning of a concept is exhausted by an analysis of one or two words. However, it is the core word and therefore will hopefully prove to be a fruitful place from which to start.

Having examined 'mission' (ie 'to send') in the NT only then will we look briefly at the story of the Bible and see the place of this theme in the wider context of biblical theology.

'Sending' in the New Testament

The expression 'to send' is commonly rendered by two words in Greek, *apostellein* and *pempein*. We will therefore briefly examine the spread of these two words in the New Testament. Is there a distinction in meaning? It is often suggested that there is. For example, Rengstorff in his analysis of *apostellein* in the *TDNT* asserts,

> We can say in general that when πέμπειν is used in the NT the emphasis is on the sending as such, whereas when ἀποστέλλειν is used it rests on the commission linked with it, no matter whether the one who sends or the one who is sent claim prior interest . . . the Synoptists never use πέμπειν but only ἀποστέλλειν of God.[4]

This distinction seems overly subtle and one wonders if the original readers understood these precise nuances in meaning! Further, while it is true that the Synoptists prefer *apostellein* when speaking of God sending his servants, there nevertheless remains some overlap in their usage of these two terms. For example, Matthew 22:1–14 records Jesus' parable of the marriage feast. On three occasions the king, who clearly represents God, sends out servants. On the first two occasions the word *apostellein* is used but on the third occasion when the king sends his soldiers the word used is *pempein*. While arguing for distinctions in meaning most scholars recognise that John is unique in using *apostellein* and *pempein* interchangeably. However, S. Zodhiates tries to see even a distinction in John: 'Therefore *pempō* is a general term, but *apostellō* suggests official

---

[4] R. Rengstorff, αποστελλω, *TDNT*, ed. G. Kittel (Grand Rapids: Eerdmans, 1964), vol.1, 404.

or authoritative sending.'[5] Mind you, earlier in his discussion of *apostellō* Zodhiates states that 'the importance of this mission is denoted by the fact that God sent His own Son'.[6] These are Paul's words from Romans 8:3. Interestingly, here the word Paul uses for God sending his son is *pempō*! My point is simply this, that while we rightly recognise one particular writer's preference for one word over another, we need to be careful about importing too much theological significance into this fact. The most significant distinction that we will draw will be between that use of 'send', be it *apostellein* or *pempein*, which is common or non-technical (for example, ('Felix sent for Paul . . . and heard him speak') and that which we can call technical ('I sent my son to preach the gospel'). By 'technical' I mean that the sending has a special purpose; people are sent to do the work of God. The context will determine whether a particular use of 'to send' is common or technical.

(1) Matthew

In our English New Testaments the first occurrence of 'sending' is found in Matthew 2.[7] Here Herod sends (*pempein*) the magi to Bethlehem (2:8). Later, he sends (*apostellein*) his soldiers to kill the male children in Bethlehem. Here is an example of how a New Testament writer can show fluidity in his use of these Greek words. These appear to be common uses of the word 'send'. The first important technical use of 'send' is found, appropriately, in the introduction to Jesus' 'Sermon on Mission' (Matt 9:35–10:42). The well known statement that 'the harvest is plentiful but the labourers are few' leads to Jesus calling on the disciples to ask the Lord of the harvest 'to send out (*ekbale*) labourers into his harvest' (9:38). Although in other parts of this sermon when Jesus speaks of sending out his apostles on their mission he uses his preferred word, *apostellein* (10:5,16,40), here he has chosen the stronger word, *ekballein*. He may well have done this to further emphasise the urgency of

---

[5] S. Zodhiates, *The Complete Word Study Dictionary, New Testament* (Chattanooga: AMG 1992) 1137.

[6] Zodhiates, 237.

[7] Matthew uses *apostellein* 21 times and *pempein* only 4.

the task. Nevertheless, this passage is a very important one as it spells out for us some aspects of Jesus' understanding of mission.

What has he sent out his apostles (*apostoloi*—10:2) to do? Jesus' compassion for crowds who are harassed and helpless without shepherds to love, protect, and guide them is the motive for this mission. The people of Israel had no shortage of shepherds, but they were like the faithless, self-serving religious leaders that the prophet Ezekiel had condemned some six centuries earlier (Ezek 34:1–10). The people of Israel needed the good shepherd of Ezek 34:11–16 who will 'feed them with good pasture . . . seek the lost . . . bring back the strayed and . . . bind up the injured'. Jesus' desire is to bring these people to himself so that he can be their good shepherd. So, he sends out his apostles to announce the coming of the kingdom that the lost sheep might be drawn to him. Jesus gives his apostles explicit instructions as he sends them out: 'Go . . . proclaim the good news . . . cure the sick, raise the dead, cleanse the lepers, cast out demons' (Matt 10:6–8).

At first sight it appears that there are two aspects to the sending of the apostles by Jesus: preaching and works of healing or compassion. This has traditionally been a justification for sending out as missionaries those who preach and those with many different kinds of works who minister to people's physical needs. This is an important text for the word versus deed debate. But is this the correct interpretation and application of the passage? Is Jesus saying that an evangelist planting churches in eastern Europe and a dentist pulling teeth in the mountains of Nepal equally reflect the dual focus of the apostolic mission? What was the purpose of the miracles in the ministry of Jesus?

While Jesus' healings and exorcisms are a reflection of his compassionate concern for the physical needs of those around him, such miraculous signs' central function was to attest to the in–breaking of the long-awaited kingdom of God in the ministry of Jesus.[8] Attempts to draw a parallel between Jesus' miracles

[8] See the helpful discussion by D. A. Carson, 'The Purpose of Signs and Wonders in the New Testament', in *Power Religion*, ed. M. S. Horton (Moody: Chicago, 1992) esp. 99–101.

and modern works of compassion falter at this point. Isaiah the prophet had prophesied that in the coming age when 'the ransomed of the Lord shall return to Zion' (Isa 35:10) then 'the eyes of the blind shall be opened, and the ears of the deaf unstopped, and the lame shall leap like a deer' (Isa 35:5,6) and good news will be brought to the oppressed (Isa 61:1). When John the Baptist had doubts whether or not Jesus was the Messiah it is to these very signs that Jesus pointed him (Matt 11:2–6). John need have no doubts that Jesus is the promised Messiah because his works testify to this fact. For this reason Jesus sends out his disciples to do these very works so that those with eyes to see may see and believe that the Messiah has come. In short, these signs pointed to the uniqueness of Jesus with the clear purpose that people believe in him and enter into his kingdom.

This is further seen in Matthew 24:24 where Jesus warns that in the future many false Messiahs will arise who will also 'produce great signs and omens'. What will be the effect of this? 'To lead astray, if possible, the elect.' Once again the purpose of signs and wonders is the same: they point to one who claims to be the Messiah and give attestation to his veracity. This is why the signs of false Messiahs are so dangerous for they, too, appear to testify to the truthfulness of this person's claim to have been sent from God.

A further distinction between Jesus' signs and modern works of compassion is found in Jesus' refusal to do signs where there was no faith. Matthew records that in Nazareth Jesus was not able to do many deeds of power 'because of their unbelief' (Matt 13:58). A modern day missionary doctor would rightly be criticised for refusing to bring medical aid to the sick on the grounds that they have only come for physical healing and give no evidence of faith. What missionary society would even send out such a person! Intrinsic to the character of modern works of compassion is their impartiality. This same impartiality is not found in the healing ministry of Jesus for the simple reason that Jesus' signs and wonders and modern ministries of healing and compassion are not the same thing. The healing ministry of Jesus pointed to the arrival of God's kingdom in his person (Matt 11:2–6).

The next significant occurrence of 'send' occurs in 15:24 where Matthew records Jesus' statement that he was sent only to the lost sheep of the house of Israel. Significantly this announcement is made in the context of the healing of the daughter of the Canaanite woman. It is in the wider context of Matthew's concern to contrast the enmity of the Jews to Jesus with the remarkable receptivity and belief of Gentiles that we must read Jesus' striking statement, 'Woman, great is your faith'. Nevertheless, Jesus is clear about the focus of his mission: he was sent by God to Israel.

Most of the remaining uses of 'sent' are found in the context of the announcement of the coming of the kingdom of heaven. In the parable of the wicked tenants (Matt 21:33–46) those who are sent are the prophets and, finally, the son. They are sent to announce the coming of the kingdom described in terms of collecting the landowner's fruit. Similarly, in the parable of the wedding banquet (22:1–14) servants are sent to invite people into the king's banquet, again a metaphor for the eschatological kingdom of heaven. In Matthew 23:34 Jesus plainly speaks of the nation's historic rejection of those 'prophets and wise men and scribes' who have been regularly sent by God. In summary, in Matthew the use of the term 'to send' is tied up with God's purpose in salvation history of sending out his messengers to announce the coming of his kingdom.

(2) Mark and Luke/Acts

The usage of the term 'sent' in Mark and Luke is of the same order as that found in Matthew.[9] Mark uses the word to speak of the sending of John the Baptist (Mark 1:2), the apostles (Mark 3:14; 6:7), and of Jesus himself (Mark 9:37). When we turn to Luke a particularly important reference is Luke 4:43 where Jesus explicitly announces the purpose of his being sent: 'I must proclaim the good news of the kingdom of God to the other cities also; for I was sent for this purpose'. What is especially significant about this statement is that it is spoken in the context of Jesus healing the crowds and the pressure upon him to continue doing that. In context his affirmation, that he was sent

[9] In Mark we find *apostellō* used 21 times and *pempō* used only once, while Luke uses the former word 26 times and the latter 10 times.

to proclaim, was equally a repudiation of the notion that he was sent to heal.

When we turn to Acts, which is so important for our understanding of mission, it is often difficult to discern what uses of *apostellein* or *pempein* should be considered technical, that is, carry some intentional theological weight in illuminating Luke's understanding of the *missio dei*, and what uses are common. In some cases a common usage is clearly intended. For example, Paul is sent (*pempein*) to the Emperor (Acts 25:21,25,27), synagogue officials send (*apostellein*) a message to Paul and his companions (13:15). As for other occurrences, it may be useful to list the contexts in which the verbs 'send' or 'are sent' occur: God sent Jesus Christ to bring times of refreshing to his people (3:20, 26); on hearing that Samaria had accepted the word of God the apostles sent Peter and John to them (8:14); Ananias is sent to Saul to restore his sight and so that he might be filled with the Holy Spirit (9:17); men are sent from Cornelius to Peter (e.g. 10:5,8,17); God sends an angel to rescue Peter (12:11); Barnabas and Saul are sent from the church in Antioch 'for the work to which (God) has called them' (13:3); the Jerusalem Council sends out men to announce its decision to the churches (15:22,25,27); Paul sends Timothy and Erastus to Macedonia (19:22);[10] God sends Paul to preach to the Gentiles (22:21; 26:17); and, finally, salvation has been sent to the Gentiles (28:28).

While one may object to the description of 'to send' in these contexts as 'technical', nevertheless it cannot escape a reader's attention that the word is always used in the context of the ministry of the gospel. This is not surprising given the purpose of the book of Acts which is to recount this very thing; the movement of the gospel from Jerusalem to Rome. But in each case those who are 'sent' serve a gospel purpose, whether it be the coming or going between Peter and Cornelius which leads to God granting to Gentiles the repentance which leads to life (Acts 11:18) or Paul and his apostolic band preaching the gospel to the Gentiles, or Judas and Silas being sent from the Jerusalem Council to

[10] Before setting off for new regions, Paul plans to return to Jerusalem. On the way he decides to visit some of the churches he has planted. Here he sends two of his co-workers ahead of him to make the necessary arrangements for his impending visit.

deliver the decision which endorses Paul's law-free gospel and so making possible the further advance of the kingdom among the Gentiles.

(3) The Johannine writings

The special contribution of John's Gospel to our understanding of mission is seen in Jesus' strong self-consciousness as the 'one sent by the Father'. On no less than forty-three occasions Jesus describes the Father as *ho pempsas me.*[11] Jesus is also clear as to the purpose of his mission: 'Indeed, God did not send the Son into the world to condemn the world, but in order that the world might be saved through him' (3:17).

The wider context of the whole Gospel indicates the character of this salvation: Jesus is the lamb of God who takes away the sin of the world (John 1:29) and those who believe in him do not perish (3:16) but receive power to become the children of God (1:12). The term 'sent' is also used of the ministry of John the Baptist (1:6—*apostellein*) and the Holy Spirit (14:26, 15:26; 16:7—*pempein*). Of particular significance is the so-called Johannine commission, 'As the Father has sent (*apestalken*) me, so I send (*pempō*) you' (20:21), which builds on Jesus' prior statement in 17:28. A great deal hangs on the interpretation of this verse. For some, this command becomes our mandate for imitating Jesus' 'holistic' mission. As his ministry included preaching and works of compassion, so he sends us to do the same works. For example, Stott argues, 'Deliberately and precisely he made his mission the *model* (emphasis his) of ours, saying

> *as* the Father sent me, *so* I send you'. Therefore, our understanding of the church's mission must be deduced from our understanding of the Son's.[12]

Stott then concludes,

> But he served in deed as well as in word, and it would be impossible in the ministry of Jesus to separate his words

---

[11] On the occasions when John records Jesus describing himself as the one sent by the father he always uses *pempō*. Otherwise he uses *pempō* (32 times) and *apostellō* (28 times) interchangeably.

[12] Stott, 23.

> from his works . . . Now he sends us, as the Father had sent him. Therefore, our mission like his, is to be one of service.[13]

We have already argued that this perspective rests on a faulty foundation. Further, we must allow the context of John's Gospel to dictate the meaning of this commission. Two things point to a narrower rather than wider focus. Firstly, we have already argued that throughout the Gospel it is emphasised that Jesus has come to save people from their sins. All the works of Jesus point to this. John explicitly tells us that his purpose in recording all these miraculous works is that people 'might believe that Jesus is the Messiah, the Son of God, and that through believing . . . might have life in his name' (John 20:31). For this reason he was sent. The narrower context of the commission points in the same direction. Having commissioned them, he proleptically gives them the Holy Spirit (20:22) and the authority to forgive or retain sins (20:23). So, they are sent and empowered to proclaim the forgiveness of sins in Jesus' name. This is of a piece with the essence of Jesus' mission throughout the Gospel. Therefore, as the Father sent the Son to bring salvation, the forgiveness of sins, new birth, freedom from condemnation, and eternal life, so the Son sends the disciples to announce and testify to these very things which are found through faith in Jesus Christ. Interestingly, Andreas J. Köstenberger, after a thorough biblical-theological analysis of 'mission' in John, reaches the same conclusion. He writes,

> The mission of the Messianic community is that of extending to unbelievers the forgiveness of sins made possible through Jesus' completed work.[14]

This usage of 'sending' is found also in the Johannine epistles. Assuming common authorship, in the space of six verses in the fourth chapter of his first epistle, John reiterates that God has

---

[13] Stott, 24.

[14] Andreas J. Köstenberger, 'The Challenge of a Systematized Biblical Theology of Mission: Missiological Insights from the Gospel of John, *Missiology* XXIII (October, 1995) 449.

sent the Son into the world. What is the purpose of this sending? 'That we might live through him' (1 John 4:9); 'to be the atoning sacrifice for our sins' (1 John 4:10); 'as the Saviour of the world' (1 John 4:14).

Finally, John in his Apocalypse uses the word *apostellein* on three occasions to refer to God sending his angel to John to make the revelation known (1:1), God's sending of the seven spirits of God (5:6), and again the sending of his angel 'to show what must soon take place' (22:6). In each case God is the one who sends and the purpose of the sending is tied up with prophetic revelation and judgment.

(4) The letters of Paul

The importance of Paul for an understanding of mission cannot be overestimated. From the now highly-esteemed work of Roland Allen, *Missionary Methods: St Paul's or Ours?*[15] at the turn of this century to the more recent investigation by Peter T. O'Brien, *Consumed by Passion: Paul and the Dynamic of the Gospel*, the inspired writings of the apostle have been seen to be definitive in identifying and describing for us the character of the Christian missionary enterprise. He is rightly seen as the first missionary theologian. His great self-consciousness is of one sent by God to preach the gospel to the Gentiles. Everything which he writes is written from this perspective and to the end that this ministry might be fulfilled.

Space does not permit an examination of Paul's missionary theology. The recent work by O'Brien, to which I have alluded, has already very competently done this.[16] All I can do is briefly outline the contexts in which Paul speaks of someone being sent. Paul is not just someone who recognises that God has sent him, but is himself a sender of others. Firstly, Paul uses 'sending' to speak of the mission of the Son (Rom 8:3; Gal 4:4), and the Spirit (Gal 4:6).[17] In 1 Cor 1:17 Paul makes explicit his understanding

---

[15] (London: World Dominion Press, 1930), Bosch (123) rightly states that amongst monographs on Paul's missiology this one occupies pride of place 'and has had a profound influence, particularly in English-speaking missionary circles'.

[16] P. T. O'Brien, *Consumed by Passion: Paul and the Dynamic of the Gospel* (Homebush West: Lancer, 1993).

of his own sending: 'For God did not send me to baptise but to preach the gospel'. This is of a piece with the popular missionary passage, Romans 10:15: 'And how are they to proclaim him unless they are sent'. Certainly Paul's purpose here is not to exhort his readers to commit themselves to the task of world evangelisation, as this text is so often and mistakenly used, nevertheless the nexus between being sent (from God) and the task of gospel proclamation which is the goal of that sending is clear. J. D. G. Dunn writes,

> The image of the preacher/herald (κῆρυς) is implicit; fundamental to Paul's conception is the preacher as spokesman for another . . . The link with ἀποστέλλειν is therefore not accidental, *since at this point the κῆρυς and the ἀπόστολος are largely overlapping concepts.*[18]

Secondly, Paul uses the 'sending' terminology when he speaks of sending his co-workers to different churches; it is striking how often his letters record such 'missions'. When we survey the contexts of these sendings we see that Paul normally has one of two purposes in mind when he sends a fellow worker. Firstly, Paul sends members of his missionary band to further teach and encourage the churches. In Romans 15:19 Paul can claim that, from Jerusalem to Illyricum, he has 'fully proclaimed the gospel'. Whatever else this intriguing statement means, at least it has reference to Paul's desire to see the establishment of mature churches. O'Brien comments,

> Proclaiming the gospel meant for Paul not simply an initial preaching or with it the reaping of converts; it included also a whole range of nurturing and strengthening activities which led to the firm establishment of congregations.[19]

This was not a work which Paul could do by himself. Therefore, we frequently find him making reference to his plans to send a co-worker to one of the churches that he has

---

17 In Rom 8:3 Paul uses the verb *pempō* while in Galatians, on both occasions he prefers *exapostellō*.

18 J. D. G. Dunn, *Romans 9–16* (Waco, Texas: Word, 1988), 621 (emphasis mine).

19 O'Brien, 43.

planted so that the believers may be built up and encouraged and so attain the maturity which was the ultimate goal of Paul's apostolic mission. In 1 Corinthians 4:17, for example, Paul announces his intention to send Timothy to the Corinthian church 'to remind you of my ways in Christ, as I teach them everywhere in every church'. In other words, Timothy will continue the teaching ministry of the apostle so that the Corinthians might grow in their imitation of Paul who is himself the model and example of Christian maturity. Similarly, Timothy was sent by Paul to the Thessalonians 'to strengthen and encourage you for the sake of your faith . . . I was afraid that somehow the tempter had tempted you and that our labour had been in vain' (1 Thess 3:2,5). On two occasions we read that Tychicus is sent to churches to inform them of the condition of the apostle and to encourage them (Eph 6:22; Col 4:8).[20] Finally, Paul wants to send his friend and fellow labourer, Epaphroditus, back to the Philippian church who first sent him with a gift for the imprisoned apostle (Phil 2:25,28; 4:16). Epaphroditus' return will have benefit for all concerned; the Philippians will be encouraged to see their old friend again and knowing their joy will relieve Paul of some anxiety he has been bearing.

In summary, each instance of Paul's sending a co-worker has to do with the ministry of the proclamation of the gospel. For the apostle Paul, mission is the work of the proclamation of the gospel. This work is wider than evangelism. For Paul proclamation is the building of the house or the planting of a garden. The first step, laying the foundation or sowing the seed, is evangelism. But a ministry of evangelism which is not followed by the labour and toil which sees the development of a mature congregation growing in Christ-likeness is as incomplete as a house in which the work has stopped when the foundation has been laid or a garden which, once prepared, is not tended with the result that it fails to bring forth fruit.

Secondly, we see Paul speaking of 'sending' in reference to the money that he collected from the Gentile churches for the

---

[20] Tychicus is also mentioned in 2 Tim 4:12 and Tit 3:12 and while Paul does not explain his reason for sending him it may well be that he will have a ministry of encouragement.

famine relief of the believers in Jerusalem. At first sight, this appears to be a use of 'sending' which gives justification to much of the missionary work which goes on today amongst impoverished peoples bringing to them relief in the forms of medical care, education, agricultural assistance, vocational training etc. While the particular character of the assistance is different, can we not say that, in essence, twentieth-century missionary works of mercy are of the same order as Paul's effort at famine relief in the first-century?

This is not the place to investigate in detail one of the most significant enterprises of Paul's missionary career. Suffice to say that Paul saw this as much more than an expression of altruistic concern for Christian brothers in need. R. P. Martin notes the heavy use of religious language in Paul's description of the collection because this work 'is invested with a sacral-liturgical aura, and never treated as a mundane secular enterprise'.[21] Drawing on earlier studies, Martin outlines the theological purpose of this collection, concluding that this resolve to come to the aid of the mother church was anchored in

> . . . his understanding of salvation-history which had at its heart the unity of the church made up of Jews and Gentiles who had entered the community of the new Israel by faith in the messiah Jesus.[22]

In other words, when Paul sends the brothers (8:18,22—*sumpempein*; 9:3—*pempein*) to Corinth to supervise the collection, he sees them as engaging in a ministry which is at the heart of his commission as the apostle to the Gentiles.

(5) The General Epistles

The writer of the Epistle to the Hebrews only uses *apostellein* on one occasion, in 1:14. Once again his use of this word is in the

---

[21] R. P. Martin, *2 Corinthians* (Waco, Texas: Word, 1986), 251.

[22] Martin, 251. P. W. Barnett plausibly speculates that the lengths which Paul went to with this collection suggests that he also saw it as an attempt to deal with Judaizers, *The Message of Corinthians* (Leicester: IVP, 1988), 140. Whether this thesis is true or not, it again highlights the close link between Paul's 'sending' people for the collection and his work as an apostle.

context of God's salvation. Speaking of the angels he describes them as 'sent to serve for the sake of those who are to inherit salvation'.

Peter in his epistles speaks of 'sending' on just two occasions. In 1 Peter 1:12 Peter speaks of the Holy Spirit 'sent (*apostalenti*) from heaven'. Once again the context makes clear that the content of the message the Spirit brought from heaven was salvation (*peri hēs sōtērias*–1:10). The second time Peter speaks of 'sending' he uses *pempein*, the word generally preferred by the NT writers for the non-technical use of sending. Here, in 2:14, Peter describes governors as sent by God to punish those who do wrong. It is doubtful whether we can draw any direct principle from this for the goal of our missionary work!

The story of the Bible

This brief survey of the 'sending' terminology in the NT has attempted to demonstrate a remarkable uniformity in its usage. Consistently, when used in a technical sense, *pempein* and *apostellein* refer to the ministry of the verbal proclamation of the gospel to the end that mature churches are planted and established. Having examined some of the NT material we can now examine the story of the Bible and see the relationship between mission and biblical theology. In his recent exhaustive analysis and critique of post-modernism, D. A. Carson devotes roughly one-third of his book to the story of the Bible and the significance of the important 'turning points' of the Bible's plot line. The context of his survey is our encounter with religious pluralism, but the methodology is equally valid for other contexts. He writes,

> But the fact remains that the Bible as a whole document tells a story, and, properly used, that story can serve as a metanarrative that shapes our grasp of the entire Christian faith.[23]

This essay can only sketch in the briefest terms the plot line of Scripture. I will highlight those significant 'turning points' as they bear on the modern understanding of mission; that

---

[23] D. A. Carson, *The Gagging of God: Christianity Confronts Pluralism* (Grand Rapids: Zondervan, 1996) 194.

missionary inclusivism which has so influenced popular and scholarly understandings of this divine imperative.

For all its depth and complexities, the story of the Bible is a remarkably simple one. The Bible opens with creation. It has frequently been noted that Genesis 1–11 serves as an introduction, not only to the book of Genesis, but to the Bible as a whole. The account of God's creation of the universe, with the special focus on his creation and exaltation of man and woman above all his creatures, and then the subsequent disobedience of the man and the woman and the catastrophic effects of the spread of sin throughout the whole human race set the scene for the rest of the biblical narrative. The important thing to notice is the universal character of these early narratives. It is the story of God and Adam; Adam being the progenitor and representative of all people. The central events of this biblical prologue—creation, the fall, the flood, and the tower of Babel—are stories that involve all humankind.

The story of the Bible in its particular focus begins with Genesis 12 and the call of Abram. While God has called out one man, through whom he will establish a special relationship and build a nation, the universal focus of God's purposes is still very much at the fore: 'and in you all the families of the earth shall be blessed' (Gen 12:3). The NRSV translation of this verse is particularly helpful as it directs our attention to the final object of God's blessing, 'all families'.[24] The Hebrew word *mîspāhăh*, rendered here 'families', denotes a fairly small group of people, smaller than a tribe.[25] Our western understanding of 'family' as the nuclear unit is unhelpful. Better perhaps is the Eastern grouping of kinship known as the *biraderi* or brotherhood, those blood relatives with whom people intermarry, share common bonds of language, customs, habits, and responsibilities. God's ultimate purpose is the blessing of these families.

What this 'blessing' entails is best understood not simply by a morphological examination of the Hebrew word *berākāh* but by examining how, in the narratives that follow, God worked out

---

[24] Compare the much less helpful rendering of the NIV, 'all nations'.

[25] See the helpful discussion in J. Piper, *Let the Nations be Glad: The Supremacy of God in Missions* (Grand Rapids: Baker, 1993), chapter 5.

this promise of blessing to the descendants of Abraham. The blessing expressed itself in his presence with them, in establishing his tabernacle, his dwelling place with them. Further, he would give them a land, one of abundance and beauty and there they would multiply and become a great nation. Their city would be the city of God and it would be glorious and impenetrable. From Jerusalem God would rule his people through his vice-regents, the judges and the kings, he would protect them from their enemies and teach them his ways so that they might walk in right paths, and so goodness and mercy would be with them all their days. These blessings would be realised on account of a mighty work of salvation that God would do for his chosen people in rescuing them from captivity to a cruel and godless nation. This event, their exodus by the mighty hand of God, would stand as a perpetual memorial of his love for them, his commitment to them, and his ultimate purpose to manifest his glory through them. This promise of blessing is worked out through the descendants of Abraham, the nation of Israel. However, while the Old Testament is primarily the story of this man's family, their walk of faith, and eventual ruin through sin, there remains a focus on the nations. In particular, the Psalms and the prophet Isaiah repeatedly point to a day when the nations will join Israel in the holy city and be taught of the Lord. All the blessings that Israel have received from the hand of God will be granted to the nations.[26]

With respect to the universal fulfilment of this purpose to bless the nations, mission scholars are virtually unanimous in their assertion that this movement in the OT is *centripetal*; the nations will be drawn to Jerusalem. This is the hope of the nations and the promise of God. The NT describes the fulfilment of this promise. All the blessings which God had promised to bestow on the descendants of Abraham, salvation and protection from enemies, land, kingship, fellowship with God find their fulfilment in the Messiah, the Lord Jesus Christ who is the Saviour of the world. Through his obedient life, atoning death, and vindication by God who raised him from death and exalted

---

[26] For example, Psalm 36:7–9; 67:1–7; 68:28–32; 72:17; 96:1–10; Isaiah 2:1–4; 18:7; 42:1–7; 45:22–23; 55:1–5.

him, a new covenant is established which embraces both Jew and Gentile.

The New Testament opens with this theme. The first detailed narrative of the NT recounts the journey of some magi, astronomers/astrologers who, beckoned by a mysterious movement of the stars, find their way to Jerusalem and, eventually, Bethlehem. There they see the Christ child and, in stark contrast to Herod and 'all Jerusalem with him' (Matt 2:3), who are disturbed by news of this birth, these pagans from a distant land present gifts to the king and worship him. While Matthew and the other Gospel writers will emphasise the nationalistic focus of Jesus' mission ('Go only to the lost sheep of the house of Israel'), the thrust of the message of the NT has been foreshadowed in this account. Between the Gospels and the rest of the NT a significant shift in movement takes place. Jesus now commands his followers to leave God's holy city and go to the nations of the world and bring them into the kingdom. The movement is now *centrifugal*. The book of Acts and its attention to the ministry and teaching of Paul describes this phenomenon and tells us of the universality of God's offer of salvation in Jesus Christ. The precise character of the blessing which God had promised to Abraham two thousand years before is also clearly revealed: it was nothing less than the gospel that the nations would be justified by faith (Gal 3:8).

The story of the Bible closes with the new creation. Once again, as with the initial act of creation, the focus is universal: men and women living in fellowship with, and under the authority of, God, in a new creation described in terms reminiscent of the Garden of Eden (Rev 22:1–5). The scenes of heaven described in Revelation remind us of the promise to Abraham:

> After this I looked, and there was a great multitude that no-one could count, from every nation, from all tribes and peoples and languages, standing before the Lamb, robed with white, with palm branches in their hands. They cried out in a loud voice saying, 'Salvation belongs to our God, who is seated on the throne and to the Lamb' (Rev 7:9–10 cf 14:6–7; 15:4; 21:3).

What, then, are the implications of the story of the Bible for our definition of mission? We have seen that God sends persons to proclaim the gospel of salvation which results in men and women coming into his kingdom. This is clearly consistent with God's purpose in creation and redemption, that people from every nation come to him and worship him. This goal is achieved as the gospel of the salvation which is found in Jesus Christ is proclaimed and the word of God is taught. This activity is what God sent the Son into the world to do, it is this activity to which the Spirit bears witness and which he empowers people to accomplish, and it is toward the fulfilment of this activity that the triune God sends men and women.

In short, the *missio dei* is the bringing of men and women to the point where they, like the magi, fall at the feet of the Christ, worship him, and offer him the gifts of praise and consecrated lives. The extent to which any Christian endeavour has this as its goal, justifies the description of that endeavour as mission. Further, it is God's purpose that men and women from every family, every tribe and every people offer God and the Lamb praise and worship in their own tongue. One of the most significant developments in modern missionary thinking has been to take the emphasis off 'reaching nations' and place it on reaching 'people groups'. So, when Jesus commanded the apostles to make disciples of all nations, *panta ta ethnē*, he really was directing them to disciple all people groups. Such an interpretation has been criticised as imposing a modern sociological analysis into the words of the ancient text and giving Jesus' words a focus and precision that he never intended. However, in defence of this interpretation of not just Matt 28:19–20, but the entire emphasis on people groups, let me say three things.

1. This interpretation of the Great Commission is understanding Jesus' intention in the light of other texts of Scripture which speak of those who are to be the recipients of the divine promise. We have seen that it was God's original intention to bless all the 'families'[27] of the earth. In the Old

[27] In the Greek translation of Genesis 12:3 and 28:14 the words, 'all the families' are translated by *pasai hai fulai*. Usually, the word *fulai* is translated in English by 'tribes'. See Piper, 182.

Testament, especially in the Psalms, the terms which we translate 'nations', 'peoples' and 'families' are used interchangeably.[28] The New Testament quotes the Abrahamic promise on two occasions. In Acts 3:25 Peter reminds his Jewish listeners that God promised, 'And in your posterity shall all the families (*pasai hai patriai*) be blessed'. Paul then quotes the Abrahamic promise in Galatians 3:6–8, saying 'in you shall the nations (*ta ethnē*) be blessed'. In other words, there is a fluidity in usage of *ethnē fulai* and *patriai* ('nations', 'tribes', 'families') but the emphasis falls on rather small ethnic groupings. In short, the modern emphasis on people groups is simply a recognition of a distinction that is present in the text. One should be wary of being overly precise in identifying what is legitimately a people group; such precision seems absent from Scripture. Nevertheless, there remains a guiding principle for modern missions: that God will be glorified by every group of people in their own tongue.

2. Today, more than at any other time, we are aware of how artificial a 'nation' can be. The nations of the world are regularly changing their composition. The demise of communism has seen the emergence of a number of new nation states. Nations are simply political groupings, often loosely bound together by a common central government. The number of liberation movements in the world point to the fact that people often feel a greater allegiance to their own ethnic group than some greater political organism. Pakistan, for example, is made up of a number of tribal groups. While people feel some sense of national identity, their true identity is found not in being part of this nation, but part of a tribal group. They will almost never marry or even socialise outside that tribal group. While in official contexts most people speak the national language, Urdu, for day to day communication people prefer the language of their hearts, their tribal language. Pakistan is only fifty years old and who knows if it will exist in its present form in another fifty years. However, there is little doubt that

---

[28] For example, Ps 96:3,7,10; 67:1–5; 108:3; 117:1; Isa 34:1.

Punjabis, Baluchis and Pathans will continue until Christ comes again. It is therefore appropriate, in our efforts to fulfil God's purpose for his creation, not just to reach Pakistan for Christ, but to seek to establish a church amongst each people group in that land.

3. Australia prides itself on being a multicultural society. It is self-confessedly a nation comprising representatives of numerous people groups. Why are churches in Sydney concerned with cross-cultural ministry? If nations understood as political groupings are an adequate target of our mission then we simply want to win 'Australians for Christ' and whether these Australians speak English or Mandarin, are black, brown, or white, is not relevant. But we see that our responsibility is wider than just Australians. The church of Jesus Christ is, in essence, not just a multi-national church but a multi-cultural church. We reflect the essential character of the church of Christ when we bring into the church people from different people groups. We do not want them to come to Christ and worship him in one *lingua franca*, say English, and with one cultural form, say Anglican. Rather we long to see people worshipping the God of the nations in their own language, and expressing this worship in appropriate ways through their cultural forms, and bringing to their understanding of God and his purposes the riches of their own cultural heritage. Our own avowed desire for cross-cultural ministry is a reflection of God's desire for people from every ethnic group in the world to be brought into his kingdom.

This, of course, has implications for the question of whether or not one has to go 'over there' to bring people into God's kingdom, or whether one can simply stay here and adequately fulfil the Great Commission. I will leave discussion of this important question until after we have concluded our examination of the meaning of mission.

Conclusions regarding 'mission'

In the light of this brief study into the meaning of mission, I want to briefly address two important and contemporary issues.

First, there is the place of works of compassion in modern missions; should missionary societies be 'sending' physiotherapists and plumbers as well as preachers and church planters? Second, there is the relative necessity of leaving one's own home in order to fulfil the missionary mandate; in other words, should the church commit itself to local mission, overseas mission, or both?

(1) Mission and works of compassion

For the past seven years I have had the privilege of serving in Pakistan with Interserve, an international, interdenominational missionary society whose stated goal is to make Christ known in word and deed. Many of the partners presently affiliated with Interserve minister to the physical needs of needy and economically depressed people. Others are involved in ministries whose purpose could be described as the verbal proclamation of the gospel and the teaching and maturing of the church. Such a neat distinction is not easily made. Many missionaries involved in works of compassion would say that it is the desire to see God's kingdom extended and churches established that primarily has motivated them to commit themselves to this work. For example, many missionary doctors serve in a mission hospital because they see medical work as a means for building bridges which can facilitate the communication of the gospel. Nevertheless, the fact remains that many missionary organisations send out personnel whose ministry is not essentially one of proclamation. What are we to say to this?

The first thing to affirm is that according to the NT 'mission' is the verbal proclamation of the gospel. Both the wider story of the Bible and a narrower investigation into the meaning and context of 'sending' in the NT points to this; God sends in order that his work of salvation might be effected and proclaimed. Anything which does not have as its defining characteristic gospel proclamation, and as its ultimate goal the bringing of men and women into God's kingdom so that they might be holy and blameless before him on the last day, is not mission.

The second thing to say is that while the term 'mission' has grown increasingly vague and amorphous in common parlance, debate about the subject can only go forward as we become clearer as to what the term really points to. For example, since we have established at Moore Theological College a Department of Mission, it is imperative that we are clear as to the purpose of this department. Such clarity comes from a proper understanding of mission. While I sincerely hope that we can provide training for Christian workers no matter what the character of their ministry will be, nevertheless the thrust of the department will be in assisting local congregations, missionary societies, churches, parachurch groups, and individuals in their work of the verbal proclamation of the gospel, and the planting and developing of mature churches.

Thirdly, all that I have said could well be seen as offensive to the many 'missionaries' who are sacrificially performing godly and loving works in the name of Christ. It need not be so. A colleague of mine in Pakistan, while on home assignment, was asked by the pastor of his local church to share in the morning service about his work. 'But tell me', said the pastor, 'what exactly do you do?' After the missionary had described his medical work the surprised pastor said, 'But how is what you're doing in Pakistan any different from what half of the people in my church are doing right now?' My friend replied that he could not see any difference. Indeed, he went on to tell me, he didn't see himself as a 'missionary'; just a Christian using his skills in a different cultural context.

On the one hand he is right: properly defined, the word 'mission' does not accurately describe the nature of his work. However, it should also be said that there is a sense in which the path of ministry which he has chosen is special and worthy of double honour. Had he stayed in his native city he could have developed a lucrative medical practice and would have been in competition with other practitioners doing this same kind of therapeutic work. Instead, he has chosen to work in an area where, to my knowledge, out of a population of about thirty million people, there would only be a tiny handful of doctors with his particular expertise. At considerable personal financial sacrifice he has chosen to work amongst the poor. He has chosen a path which has involved much personal and emotional sacrifice, including long periods of separation from his family. Out of his love for Christ and in the name of Christ this man is compassionately seeking to alleviate the suffering of people in a needy, poorly developed country. The word one should rightly use to describe such a ministry is not 'mission'; the NT does not speak of mission in such a broad sense. But that is not to denigrate the glory or the importance of such work.

One criticism that can be levelled at we who define mission narrowly is that, in our zeal to see the gospel spread, we can appear disparaging of those who minister to people's physical needs. This criticism is often warranted. Too often we are heard to be saying that the only work of real value or eternal value is the work of gospelling. Other works, while laudable, are expendable; indeed, given our limited resources we ought to be concentrating on the work of proclamation. I believe that such a sentiment is uncharitable and unbiblical. Works of compassion done in the name of Christ are intrinsically good. We are to do good to all people, although the household of faith has the priority. The parable of the Good Samaritan stands as a perpetual reminder to us of the approval God gives to those who see a neighbour in physical need and reach out to meet that need. The Australian church is a wealthy church; we can well afford to support and endorse both those involved in mission, that is, gospel proclamation through which churches are planted and nurtured, and those involved in works of compassion.

The fact that I believe that it is helpful to distinguish two different kinds of work does not mean that I wish to denigrate the importance of Christian works of charity. To the contrary, I want to allow works of compassion to stand on their own right. A doctor should not have to feel that they are also involved in evangelism in order to give their medical work integrity in the eyes of the church. The work itself stands as one that is intrinsically pleasing to God. We will exhort this person, as we exhort each and every believer, to live lives which adorn and commend their Christian confession and to 'give a reason for the hope that is in them' as the opportunity arises, but we need to affirm works of compassion, indeed work generally, as inherently good and pleasing in the sight of God.

I am, therefore, not endorsing the sacred/secular dichotomy that is so common in much popular Christian thinking. 'Full-time ministry' or work that is church-related is 'spiritual', and therefore merits God's special favour, and 'ordinary', nine-to-five employment is 'secular', with the implication that it has no special significance. This dichotomy is a false one. All that a believer does, he or she does for the glory of God. 'Moreover', as the Preacher reminds us, 'it is God's gift that all should eat and drink and take pleasure in all their toil' (Eccl 3:12–13). Nevertheless, one can draw two false conclusions from this. Since work, and in particular works of compassion, is good and laudable then we can play fast and loose with language and apply the word 'mission' to every act of service. We have seen that it is clear from the NT that every disciple was not concerned with mission. That is, every disciple was not sent to contribute to the work of furthering the verbal proclamation of the gospel. So, we ought to retain the word 'missionary' and keep it distinct from other words like 'disciple', 'servant', or 'world citizen'.

Secondly, arguing that the secular/spiritual divide is unwarranted and recognising the intrinsic worth of labour must not be construed to mean that all works that are done to the glory of God are equal in importance. This egalitarianism may sound politically correct but it lacks Scriptural support. Paul could exhort people to strive for the 'greater gifts' (1 Cor 12:31). Greatness here is understood in terms of the extent to which some gifts bring edification to the body of Christ. While all are one in Christ Jesus, and we are to esteem the least in the body of Christ (in itself a suggestion that there should not be a levelling in the worth of spiritual gifts), there are still those whose ministry is more significant for the growth of the church. In Ephesians 4, while acknowledging that each person has received gifts of grace, Paul particularly affirms that it is the apostles, prophets, evangelists, pastors and teachers who play the primary role in building up and equipping the saints (Eph 4:7–13). So, those who are sent to preach and teach have a ministry which ought to be recognised to be of special significance. Mission is not everything we do. We are not all missionaries. Both these concepts have a particular focus in the Scriptures and the work of mission has a position of importance that ought not to be diminished.

One could ask, if mission is proclamation then ought not missionary societies send out gospel preachers and teachers and leave those who wish to be involved with ministries of helps to pursue other avenues, say with one of the many Christian charitable organisations, or some government body? It may be appropriate for a society to do this. If the society is committed to mission in the traditional understanding of the word, then it may well commend to prospective candidates who do not share this same burden those fine Christian organisations who exist to minister to the vast physical needs of the world's people. On the other hand, at this point one may choose to be practical. Missionary societies have established the infrastructures, expertise, and reputation which makes possible the advancement of both gospel ministries and works of charity in many different nations. It may be foolish to forsake all this. The last thing the church needs is more organisations!

(2) Local mission, overseas mission, or both?

The second matter concerns the question of local mission versus overseas mission. At a popular level there seems to be considerable confusion over this point. I recently heard a Christian leader confess that she wasn't sure why one had to travel to another country to do missionary work when there is so much to be done here. 'Still,' she said, 'God's ways are often mysterious.' This person believes in and supports foreign missionaries; she's just not really sure why! Indeed, the more I talk with mission-minded people the more I find that this is a question for which they usually do not have an answer. Sydney is a city of nearly four million people, the vast majority of whom are unconverted. Given all the expense and difficulty involved in moving to a distant culture, it does appear foolish to take people out of effective ministries in their own country and transport them to a situation where everything will be unfamiliar and where there will be many more barriers to effective evangelism.

What is our response? The first thing to affirm is that, even cross-culturally, ministry here in Sydney provides us with many unique opportunities. We have already argued that God's purpose for his creation is not just the salvation of individuals but the salvation of men and women from every tribe, people, and tongue. Therefore, a commitment to cross-cultural ministry is not an optional extra for us. In the providence of God, Australia, like other Western nations, has seen an influx of immigrants in recent years. Australia finds herself in a unique position to minister to people from other cultures, especially Asia. Firstly, we have a regional affiliation with Asia. While most Asians do not see Australia as part of Asia[29] and culturally, historically, and linguistically we are not, Australia is consciously moving towards Asia. Asianisation will be at least a part of whatever comprises our future national identity. Secondly, despite all the bad press Australia has been receiving lately regarding racism, Aussies are by and large a tolerant people. Stephen FitzGerald comments,

> In terms of parliamentary democracy, and the rule of law, and the basic freedoms, and equality, and the liberalism and humanism of our democratic tradition, Australia has the most open and tolerant society in the region.[30]

This context provides the Australian church with a God-given 'moment' to reach across the barriers to people of other traditions, cultures, and faiths with the message of the gospel of Jesus Christ.

So, the Australian church must commit itself to local cross-cultural mission. The question remains: if I can preach the gospel cross-culturally right here in Sydney, why leave familiar territory? The basic answer is a simple one: the fact remains that many of the people groups in the world will not be reached unless people are prepared to cross cultural boundaries. Australians have the personnel, the financial resources, and a good international reputation, all of which mean that we should be deeply involved in the world wide task of gospel proclamation and the developing of mature churches. That is not all. We are a spiritually rich church. We have many pastors and lay leaders who are amongst the most biblically literate and theologically qualified in the world. Seminaries and Bible colleges in other countries can greatly benefit from the expertise

---

[29] S. FitzGerald, *Is Australia an Asian Country?* (Sydney: Allen & Unwin, 1997), 9. He comments, 'I know of few East Asians who say with no reservation at all that Australia belongs to their region, however they define it. They may like individual Australians, and some who have been here may even like Australia. But they do not regard it as being a part of what they are'.

[30] FitzGerald, 70.

and fellowship of Australian evangelical theological educators. At one stage each of the three major seminaries in Pakistan had on its staff, either full-time or part-time, a graduate from Moore Theological College. Through their ministries these people made significant contributions to the strengthening of the desperately needy local Pakistani church. Colleges like Moore should be actively pursuing means whereby they can support churches in countries which are lacking such resources and ought to be regularly exposing their students to these needs and challenging them to 'go'.

However, without diminishing the urgency of this task and how imperative it is that Australian churches commit themselves to this task, I do want to raise one or two caveats. Firstly, there is a lot of pietistic nonsense around about overseas missionary work. I have heard it said that we should send foreign missionaries even if there is no work for them to do, because their presence in another culture is a witness to the multi-cultural character of the body of Christ. When we hear of the U.S.A. spending millions of dollars to send missionaries to Korea or Japan and then Koreans or Japanese spending similar sums to send missionaries to America then one wonders, 'Where has Christian prudence and common sense gone?' One cannot imagine multi-national companies spending their money in such a way; indeed, 'the children of this age are more shrewd in dealing with their own generation than the children of light' (Luke 16:8).

Further, one ought not to underestimate the difficulties in effective cross-cultural communication. Preaching the gospel in a language which is not your own is not the preferred method for effective evangelism. One may learn a new language, although for the average cross-cultural worker, that in itself is a task which can take many years before real proficiency is attained. That is only the beginning. I remember speaking with a fellow-worker in Pakistan, himself the son of missionaries, who had been born and brought up in the host culture. Paul was fluent in the language, culturally at ease with people of the country, and sincerely appreciative of much of the culture. Yet even he was not, in the purest sense of the word, bi-cultural. He confessed that just when he would begin to think that he was on the wavelength of the people someone would say or do something which reminded him that there is an enormous gulf in how his home culture and his host culture perceived reality. It is in recognition of this fact that Theological Education by Extension demands that all of its courses in Pakistan, if written by an expatriate, be written by the expatriate in his mother tongue and then translated by a Pakistani. No matter how proficient the foreigner might be in his second language, TEE rightly acknowledges that no-one can communicate biblical truths with the understanding and accuracy of someone who is indigenous to the country.

Modern missiologists like Ralph Winter have recognised this fact. They identify three kinds of evangelism, E-1, E-2, and E-3. E-1 evangelism is local evangelism in which there are no cultural barriers to be crossed in order to communicate the gospel. E-2 is akin to a first century Jew speaking to a Samaritan. While they may share considerable linguistic and cultural habits, there are still significant cultural differences between them. E-3 is speaking to those whose language, ways of thinking, and cultural patterns are very different from those of the communicator. Winter rightly observes that 'the national leader always has a communication advantage over the foreigner'.[31] If we wanted to reach English speaking Aussies of an Anglo-Saxon background who would we ask to do it? Koreans? Kenyans? Some even think that Americans are too distant culturally! No, we would seek an Australian; one who is linguistically and culturally at one with the people he or she is trying to reach. As a general principle the closer a person is culturally to the target people group the more likely he or she is to be effective.

One could say a great deal more about this, but this will have to suffice. There is a challenge to our churches to commit themselves to cross-cultural mission both locally and globally. There is also a call for churches and sending agencies to be wise and strategic in the placement of personnel and in how they fulfil these missions.

---

[31] R. Winter, 'The New Macedonia', in *Perspectives on the World Christian Mission*, eds, R. D. Winter and S. C. Hawthorne (Pasadena: William Carey Library, 1981) 300.

Defining 'Missiology'

Given the endemic confusion about the meaning of 'mission' it would be a little surprising if the study of mission, or 'missiology', suffered any less in its search for a definition. Sadly scholars seem unable to agree on any precise parameters for this term. James A. Scherer begins by acknowledging that, up until now, 'the quest for an agreed definition of *missiology* remains elusive'.[32] Twenty pages later he concludes that such a definition will probably continue to elude us. Perhaps this isn't surprising given that the study of missiology embraces so many academic disciplines. Missiologists were once colourfully described as 'lost sheep ... scattered among the folds of history, theology, comparative religions, and education, wandering from the theological field to the practical and back again'.[33]

What is Missiology?

A definition of 'missiology' must be closely related to our understanding of the nature and purpose of 'mission'. If mission is the sending of someone to proclaim the gospel so that a mature church might be planted and grown then fundamentally the study of this work is the concern of missiology. As we seek to describe the essence of missiological study it is helpful to go back to the beginnings of the establishment of the study of mission as an academic discipline. While the title 'the father of missiology' is usually bestowed upon Gustav Warneck, who in 1897 was appointed to the chair of the 'science of mission' at Halle University in Germany, the birth of missiology as a science came thirty years earlier in Scotland. In 1867 the great Scottish missionary, Alexander Duff, was appointed professor of Evangelical Theology at the Free Church College in Edinburgh. On the occasion of his election to this chair, Duff in his address said,

> When passing through the theological curriculum of St. Andrews, I was struck markedly with this circum-

[32] J. A. Scherer, 'Missiology as a Discipline and What It Includes', in *New Directions in Mission and Evangelization* eds. J. A. Scherer and S. B. Bevans (Maryknoll: Orbis, 1994) 175.

[33] J. L. Dunstan, quoted by Scherer, 176.

> stance, that throughout the whole course of the curriculum of four years not one single allusion was ever made to the subject of the world's evangelization—the subject which constitutes the chief end of the Christian Church on earth.[34]

Duff's goal was to challenge the whole church with the 'magnitude and glory of the work of the world's evangelization'. He did this tirelessly in the pulpits of the Church of Scotland but he also saw the strategic value of a professorship of 'Missions and Education' at the college where men trained for the ministry. In his own words its purpose would be

> to infuse the missionary spirit into the minds of our students and young ministers, and through them into the minds of the people, and to secure a larger supply alike of men and pecuniary means.[35]

It is striking, as one reads of the establishment of that first chair in mission, how the issues that that fledgling department faced are the same issues that Moore College faces today as we seek to establish a department. Firstly, should the focus of such a chair or department be home missions or foreign missions? Duff, rightly, drew no sharp distinction between the two. They both constituted the one essential task: evangelization. Although Duff, while a missionary in India, worked tirelessly in establishing a medical college, a hospital, and a network of schools for Indians, he nevertheless would have concurred with our definition of mission. For him 'evangelistic' and 'missionary' were synonymous. Consequently, whether at home or abroad the task of evangelization was the same. So, it is this same dual concern that drives our new department. We desire to inform and equip men and women for the ministry of gospelling here at home amongst people of other cultures. At the same time we want to motivate many to take the message to those who have not heard, who live beyond the borders of our city, or to work

---

[34] Quoted in O. G. Myklebust, *The Study of Missions in Theological Education* Vol.1 (Oslo: Olson, 1955; 2 vols) 168. Myklebust's two-volume study remains the definitive work on the origins and development of the study of missions.
[35] Quoted in Myklebust, 190.

with those churches who lack the resources that God has graciously endowed us with in this diocese that we might together strive to bring the church throughout the world to spiritual maturity.

Given that missiology 'wanders across the folds' of various disciplines, the question must be raised as to where it fits in; what is its relationship with the other disciplines. In American seminaries it is often found detached from the traditional theological disciplines. Schools of World Mission are now common: separate entities in fellowship with the mainline faculties but limited in their opportunities for cross-fertilisation. Moore College has chosen, rightly, not to take this course. Ours is a department which must stand alongside its older brothers of 'Biblical Studies', 'Christian Thought', and 'Ministry'. It has common ties with each of these departments. The foundation of missiology is found in the Bible and therefore careful exegesis of Scripture must be the first task of the missiologist. At the same time missiological study is also firmly grounded in Christian history. The missiologist must understand the historical framework and have a grasp of the background to the contemporary issues as well as drawing valuable lessons from the two thousand years of missionary endeavour.

It is upon these two pillars of biblical studies and Christian thought that a firm missiological study must be based. However, the discipline is also inherently and necessarily practical; it seeks to equip its students for the task of world evangelization. So, it is appropriate that missiology studies and critiques the religions of the world. Further, insights drawn from the social sciences, filtered through the grid of Scripture, assist us in our cross-cultural communication and our endeavours in church planting. Alexander Duff recognised these two sides of mission study. It was his desire to teach the more general, or what I have termed foundational, subjects in the college curriculum and then establish a missionary institute for training in the more practical subjects.

In summary, Alexander Duff rightly understood that the focus of missiological study is the evangelisation of the world and that the pillars on which this study rests are the Bible and theology. Lest all this strike us as obvious, it is alarming to see the extent to which missiology has gone adrift from its proper and original moorings. The great tragedy of modern missiology is that those disciplines which ought to be setting its agenda and informing its thinking have been marginalised. Biblical studies and Christian thought, in particular theology and church history, occupy positions on the fringes of missiological thought. Conversely, those disciplines which ought to belong as adjuncts to the course, worthy of study and the gleaning of wisdom but unworthy of any authoritative status and inappropriate for determining the nature and focus of mission, have become the pillars and agenda-setters for the study and practice of mission. I am referring to the social sciences, in particular anthropology, psychology, sociology and linguistics.

A survey of missiological journals

The degree to which social science and missiological praxis, as opposed to biblical studies and theology, determines missiological thought is evidenced by the contents of three of the leading missiological journals. The articles published by these journals over the last ten years alert us to the key issues with which missiologists are grappling these days and, by implication, those issues which they see as most significant for the study of mission. They also indicate which academic disciplines are most influencing missiological thought, and therefore by extension, missionary practice.

Missiology is the quarterly journal of the American Society of Missiologists. It began in 1973, incorporating the journal *Practical Anthropology*. So, from the beginning, its special interest was the social sciences. In his guest editorial for the first issue, Gerald Anderson stated that the purpose of the new journal was to 'provide more resources toward better understanding and effectiveness in the Christian mission'.[36] He went on to say

> . . . the scope of concerns . . . includes the pooling of knowledge, skills, and techniques provided by the social and behavioural sciences, regional area studies, and by a wide range of practical professions such as agriculture,

[36] G. Anderson, *Missiology* 1 (1973) 3.

> education, medicine, and public health as well as theological studies and devoted Christian witness in all its forms'.[37]

The range of articles over the past 10 years indicates that this indeed has been the scope of *Missiology* (see Table 1). My division of articles according to their subject matter is somewhat artificial. Many authors draw upon a variety of academic disciplines in the writing of an article. For example, the article 'Robert DeNobili, Adaptation, and the Reasonable Interpretation of Religion' draws upon history as it deals with issues concerning dialogue with world religions. I have placed this article under 'history'. 'Mission Studies' is something of a 'catchall' embracing those issues which are of special pertinence to missiology like 'the gospel and the poor', pentecostal missions, and so forth.

The breadth of interest of *Missiology* is wide, enveloping the broad span of subjects that come under the orbit of missiology. There are serious discussions of issues relating to dialogue with other religions as well as discussions of more practical matters to do with missionary life. As the table indicates, the social sciences are the most significant influence on missiological studies. *Missiology* has published some fine articles which examine missiological issues from a biblical perspective, but they comprise less than 5% of all articles published. The other articles, many of which deal with issues on which the Bible has a good deal to say, are nevertheless written with little or no reference to the perspective of the Scriptures. We have seen that from the beginning the editors of the journal did not mention biblical studies as one of the pools from which knowledge and skills for effective Christian world mission would be gathered (although presumably biblical studies was subsumed under 'theological studies'). Still, it gives one cause to wonder when explicitly the findings of agriculture and public health are deemed to be more fruitful sources for illumination in to how we might fulfil the Great Commission than the church's Scriptures!

The most widely read and influential missiological journal is the *International Bulletin of Missionary Research (IBMR)*. Once

[37] Anderson, 4.

Table 1: Analysis of articles in *Missiology*

Subject	*No. of articles*	*% of total*
Social Sciences	67	23.8
Biblical Studies	14	5.0
Contextualization	19	6.7
Reports	8	2.9
Gospel & Culture	20	7.1
World Religions	28	10.0
Case Studies	21	7.5
Mission Studies	67	23.8
Mission History	23	8.2
Missionary Life	3	1.1
Spirituality, Ecumenism, Christology, Women	11	3.9

Table 2: Analysis of articles in *IBMR*

Subject	*No. of articles*	*% of total*
Contextualization	8	3.4
Descriptive	40	17.0
Mission History	77	32.7
Personal Testimony/Reflection	46	19.6
Statistical Tables	23	9.8
Reports/Reviews	15	6.4
Dialogue/World Religions	16	6.8
Miscellaneous[38]	10	4.3
Biblical Studies	0	0.0

again I have surveyed the spread of articles over the past 10 years.

The *IBMR* is a helpful missiological journal and its ongoing commitment to the study of mission history makes it a valuable resource for missiologists. However, the fact that there has been no serious investigation of any missiological subject from a biblical-theological perspective is a telling indictment, not just on this journal, but on the whole of missiological study. Twenty years ago the journal began (as the Occasional Bulletin of Missionary Research) and in its first issue in January 1977, the editor outlined the journal's major areas of concern. They would include the history and theology of mission, contemporary

---

38 'Miscellaneous' includes ecumenical apologetics, mission historiography, African theologies, ethnocentrism and so on.

problems in missionary life and work, issues of language and culture in mission, relating the gospel to the sociopolitical realities, development of indigenous churches and theologies, and understanding and communicating with persons of other faiths.[39] These are surely topics on which the Bible has something to say. The Scriptures ought to be directing our thoughts.

The *IBMR* is a journal written for, and by, missiologists from a broad spectrum of theological traditions. From an avowedly evangelical position comes the popular *Evangelical Missions Quarterly*. This journal is designed to assist those working in cross-cultural ministry. The contributors are both mission directors and those 'on the field', writing and speaking out of their own experiences and reflections. Its emphasis is on the practical, with many of the articles being case studies in which mission practitioners share insights they have gleaned over years of cross-cultural service. One would have expected a journal which announces itself as 'evangelical' to have displayed this in the place it gives to Scriptures in the articles it publishes. I have found it impossible to categorise the types of articles published in *EMQ*, as they cover a wide range of subjects. For example, in the most recent issue that I consulted, April 1997, there were articles on recruiting missionaries, church planting, missionary children, information technology, partnership, and prayer. There have been some 312 articles published by *EMQ* in the ten years prior to 1997 and only 5 of them could be considered a biblical study. This amounts to 1.6% of all articles. Of these five, some could not be considered a serious attempt at a biblical analysis of missionary practice, for example, 'If Paul got Organized so could you: administrators and missionaries can manage their lives according to disciplines developed by the Apostle Paul'.[40] Such articles make little attempt to seriously interact with the text of Scripture and often amount to little more than proof-texting.

In a journal that is avowedly evangelical and whose subject matter is world mission, it is a sad commentary on the state of evangelical missionary thinking, analysis, and research that the

---

[39] L. Golz, 'If Paul got organised, so can you', *EMQ* 27 (1991) 268–272.
[40] *EMQ*, vol 27, 1991.

Bible is seen to have little to say to us. The findings of the social sciences and case studies from the field are seen to be more influential and worthy of reflection than serious study of theology and the Bible. One can only assume that in evangelical missiological thinking if we want to be practical in our writing about missions, then we will have to put the Bible to one side and listen, instead, to wisdom gleaned from observation and experience. It is not surprising then that *EMQ* is consistently and uniformly shallow in its discussion of missiological issues. In the context of his discussion about the demise of theology in American evangelical thinking David Wells observed, 'As theology moved from the center to the periphery of evangelical faith, technique moved from the periphery to the center'.[41] The same indictment could be levelled against modern missiology and its marginalisation of those disciplines which are its very foundation.

Back to the Bible: returning missiology to its theological foundation

Amidst this bleak picture of the state of missiological research, there are a few encouraging signs. Gradually, there appears to be a recognition that we ought to allow the Scriptures to inform our thinking about mission. Not only has this sprung from a general unease in some circles that the social sciences ought not to be determining missionary thinking as much as they do at present, but also the degree to which a great deal of modern writing on missions by evangelicals is biblically uninformed. In this compendium, Phillip Jensen explores the intrinsic relationship that exists between much thinking on church growth and secular marketing theory. When one reads of articles in *Missiology* with titles such as 'Choosing a Church Planting Strategy that Works'[42] then we are reminded how much missionary thinking and practice reflects a disturbing confidence in human thinking and methods at the expense of the plans and purposes of a sovereign God.

---

[41] D. Wells, *God in the Wasteland* (Grand Rapids: Eerdmans, 1994) 71.
[42] *Missiology* XXIV (1996).

One could also point to the rampant triumphalism in modern missionary thinking. Comments like the following reflect much of the thinking behind today's 'AD 2000 Movement': '(I am) looking forward to seeing historical, unprecedental, monumental, supernatural and global revival to fulfil the Great Commission in this generation'.[43] When C. Peter Wagner boldly claims that 'the 1990's is now seeing the greatest spiritual harvest in history'[44] we really have to ask, 'how does he know?'. Because the statistics from the latest survey by David Barrett tell him? Certainly, there are encouraging stories of many coming to Christ in China, South Korea, Africa, and South America but we must let the sober realism of the Scriptures inform and control the unbounded enthusiasm of much popular missiological thinking and reporting. Jesus asked the disciples, 'When the Son of Man comes will he find faith on earth?' I think that our Lord expected the reply, 'not much'. Wagner would presumably respond, 'You bet, and lots of it!'. Our Lord warned that in the last days the love of many will grow cold. If the church growth enthusiasts are to be believed then this spiritual ice age is past and now we're basking in a heat wave.

The emphasis on human strategising and planning apart from any serious interaction with the Scriptures is also evidenced in the false dichotomy between the 'theoretical' and the 'practical' that is heard so much today. Prospective ministry and missionary candidates are regularly heard to say that they want a course of study which is more practical than theoretical. It is implied that if people want to win the world for Christ then they do not need more theology or more Bible study, but that they need courses of study that will practically equip them for this task. It is the social sciences and personal case studies that will provide this practical equipment.

What can be said about this? Firstly, this is an implicit diminishing of the authority of Scripture. The assumption seems to be that the Scriptures teach us about the way of salvation but when

---

[43] Quoted by L. Bush in 'Global Consultation on World Evangelization', *Global Church Growth* XXX1 (1994) 7.

[44] C. P. Wagner, 'The AD 2000 and Beyond Movement' in *Global Church Growth* XXIX (1992) 9.

it comes to the means of bringing this salvation to the world it is only one voice amongst many and a voice that is increasingly muted. One needs only look at Paul's missionary practice to see the extent to which the gospel, rooted in the Old Testament and the life and teaching of Jesus, informed his thinking about his missionary work. In this regard Paul is rightly our missionary model. Allowing the gospel to critique and inform our praxis is hardly impractical. Consequently, the more we study the gospel and its implications then the more we will understand the will of God regarding matters of our missionary practice.

It should be said, that biblical scholars themselves must shoulder some of the blame for the development of this unhelpful bifurcation. So often their exegesis and exposition of the text stops at the point of explaining its meaning in its original context and does not proceed to elucidating its meaning and implications for contemporary Christian life and practice. In so doing we unwittingly give the impression that the Bible is an authority on matters of biblical history and Christian doctrine but rarely impinges on modern life. Biblical scholars who are missiologists need to be marrying faithful exegesis of the Scriptures with an informed understanding of current missiological issues. Secondly, I am not trying to perpetuate the dichotomy by replacing an emphasis on the so-called practical with an emphasis on the theoretical. The dichotomy itself is a false one. The serious study of the Bible and theological reflection on the Bible is eminently practical. We recognise that other disciplines inform and help us as we seek to cross cultures with the message of salvation. However, these disciplines must be studied under the supervising authority of the Scriptures.

The need of the hour in missiological studies is to return the discipline to its proper theological foundations. In this regard Moore College can play a strategic role. Notice, I do not say the 'Moore College Department of Mission'. This new department is not an organism in isolation from the other disciplines. We are part of a larger body and together, through our mutual cross-fertilisation, we enrich and enhance our own studies. Moore College's commitment to the doctrines of the Reformed faith and its emphasis on biblical theology as the proper means of understanding and applying the Scriptures, guarantees that this college can bring to missiological studies a perspective which is sorely needed.

The hour of opportunity

I have alluded to the fact that the distinctive biblical-theological emphases of Moore College, which inform the direction of thinking of all the College disciplines, and therefore will also inform the Department of Mission, give the College the potential to make a significant contribution to missiological studies. At the same time, this department is being established at a strategic moment in the history of the Anglican Diocese of Sydney and its commitment to world evangelisation.

A Department of Mission has been established at Moore College because we recognise the theological importance of missiology; that our God is a missionary God and that the story of salvation-history is a story of mission. At the same time pragmatic factors have also propelled the college in this direction. The world has come to our city. Indeed, the nations of the world are changing the face of our city. If we are to be obedient to the biblical mandate to make disciples of all nations and if our church is to grow then we need to find ways and means of communicating Christ to these nations who now live cheek by jowl with us.

We have already examined the theological imperative for committing ourselves to cross-cultural evangelisation. However, how we fulfil this imperative in our present context is one of the great challenges facing our denomination. We are part of a nation confused about its identity. Politically and economically we are seeking to be part of a region whose dominant histories, cultures and ethical and value systems we do not share or understand. FitzGerald colourfully describes Australia as

> . . . a Europe-derived culture in a sea of Asian cultures, ruled by a transplanted European people soaking up the sun and skin cancer in a climate for which they were never intended.[45]

---

[45] FitzGerald, 57.

We are a nation whose acknowledged cultural heritage is European but who sees its future identity with Asia. This presents a significant challenge to denominations like our own whose cultural and ecclesiastical heritage is also very much tied to Europe. The forms of our worship are European. The nature of how we relate to one another is European. The language of our worship is European. How we contribute to the reaching of these nations given our European heritage and traditions is one of the urgent challenges facing our church and therefore this department.

At the same time, we are seeing in these days graduates of Moore College working independently of traditional church structures, seeking to plant churches in the towns and cities of Australia where there is little ministry which reflects the Reformed, biblical-theological emphases of this college. Preparing future students for such a ministry and equipping and assisting those presently engaged in church planting is another challenge this department faces.

The Department of Mission also provides us with the forum for an intellectual interface with our society. The demise of modernism and the emergence of post-modernism as the dominant worldview of late twentieth century western society has been well documented. It is imperative that Moore College provide a lead in both understanding this new intellectual development and help Christians understand how the gospel can be communicated in such a pluralistic framework.

Along with these new endeavours, the Department of Mission ought to challenge, inform, stimulate, and equip men and women for ministry across cultures, especially outside of Australia. Moore College has consistently seen its graduates involved in a wide range of strategic gospel ministries throughout the world. The establishment of a fully-fledged department can only hope to provide for those graduates better training and resourcing.

These tasks are challenging and daunting but, returning to the point made at the beginning of this article, mission is the *missio dei*. It is the work of God, springing from him, empowered by him, and ultimately brought to its completion by him. It is in this confidence that Moore College and the Department of Mission seeks to fulfil its mandate.

Exploring further

1. 'The Bible's fundamental theme is mission'. Do you agree?
2. Should missionary societies support those whose work does not serve the work of the verbal proclamation of the gospel?
3. Can you be a missionary in word and not deed? Can you be a missionary in deed and not word?
4. What contribution can the social sciences make to our study of mission?
5. If you were to start a 'department of mission' what would you consider to be its core subjects? Justify your choices.